John Crawford

Photo Credits

Cover photo of Indian Hill taken by Judy Crawford

Aerial photos of Slims Fire taken by Bill Wilkinson

Picture of the author looking for smokes out on the catwalk in 2022 taken by Jason Freeze

Ray Kresek took photo of author feeding Golden-Mantled Ground Squirrel at Coolwater

Photo of author on page 205, and photos of eagles on page 228 taken by Joe Gordon

Upper picture on page 208 taken by a visitor, whose name I don't recall

Gary Winek took the picture on page 231

Back cover photo of Sundance taken by author

Photos of the author on pages 66, 67, 113, 119, 122, and 125 taken by Judy Crawford

All other photos taken by author

Above It All

By John Crawford

Copyright © 2022 by John Crawford

ISBN: 978-1-938707-63-6

Library of Congress Control Number:
2023901788

Published in Stevensville, Montana, United States of America

First Edition

ALL RIGHTS RESERVED
No part of this publication can be reproduced, stored in a retrieval system, or transmitted by any form or by any means without the prior written consent of the author or publisher.

STONEYDALE PRESS PUBLISHING CO.
523 Main Street • PO Box 188
Stevensville, Montana 59870
406-777-2729 • 1-800-835-7006
www.stoneydale.com

"I went to the woods because I wished to live deliberately, to front only the essential facts of life, and see if I could not learn what it had to teach, and not, when I came to die, discover that I had not lived."

Henry David Thoreau

In my case, you can substitute "I went to the <u>mountaintop</u> because I wished to live deliberately…"

Acknowledgments

I would like to thank Judy for giving up the comforts of civilization to live on Indian Hill for 22 wonderful summers together. Also, thanks for giving me valuable suggestions for my book.

I am appreciative of all the people who have supported and encouraged my writing...my friends Gary Winek, Kris and Bob Anderson, Stan Benes, Bo and Cindy Lane, John and Kathy Clark, Tom Vandewater, Pam Aunan, Ray Kresek, Carol Taylor, and Joyce Wallinder. Thanks to Lorie Palmer Russell, a reporter for the Idaho County Free Press, for encouraging me to write a lookout book. Also a big thank you to Julie Pallas, Dr. Brett Felton, and Gina Blahmik-Elliott of Felton Dental Care in Missoula, for their support of my writing endeavors over the years. And thanks to all the Lolo businesses who have supported the selling of my past books; Lolo Harvest Foods, Lolo Drug, and the Sweets Barn. Thanks, Dr. Dessye Dee Clark, for always being a cheerleader of my writing ambitions. And I really appreciate the support of my church "family".

A big thank you to my sister, Carol Massat, who has always been a big moral support.

Much appreciation to my proofreader, Tanna Paulson, for spending countless hours editing all my books.

And I especially want to thank Rachel Burk, of Stoneydale Press in Stevensville, for publishing <u>Above It All.</u>

Note From the Author

When I finally decided in the spring of 2021 to get a lookout book published, after 45 seasons as a fire spotter, I already had the 1998 and 2001 Indian Hill, and 2020 Sundance Lookout journals written as the events happened in those respective years. Deciding to include Judy's and my inaugural Indian Hill season in 1974, I didn't have any journal notes to refer to when writing that chapter in our lives. So the 1974 lookout journal is written from our collective memories. All the dates in that story are approximate, except for June 22nd, July 4th, August 11th, September 15th, and October 19th. We remembered that we had quite a few storms that first season on lookout, but I write about only one that is especially engrained in our memories...the biggest storm we ever had on lookout.

This book is dedicated to all the lookouts who keep a vigil for forest fires every season across this land, and to the brave wildland firefighters who put them out.

Foreword

Very often in our day-to-day lives, we tend not to think of the people and places that quietly exist doing paramount work. A fire lookout is a prime example. Perched up in the mountains, the lookout crews living in fire lookout towers spend each day on high alert, looking for wildfires and rushing to relay the information that could mean saving the forests and saving lives. It's just not an everyday thought for most of us, the work that a lookout must do – but that is not the case for John Crawford. Since 1974, John has been working as a lookout in the wilds of northern Idaho. In this memoir, John shares his experiences and adventures of those years working and living in the towers.

John Crawford, who lives in Lolo, Montana, is no stranger to writing books – he authored three books prior to this one. In his first book, *The Woodman Echo: 1892-1992*, John penned about the old school that was built in the Lolo Creek Canyon, west of Lolo, Montana, on the old wagon road. This log cabin, a one-room school, was originally built on a homestead in 1892. In 1902, a new school was erected about a quarter mile east of this little log cabin. This school is still in use today. His second book, *Lewis & Clark and me...Heading West from Travelers' Rest,* documented his own personal journey along the Lewis and Clark Trail and the knowledge he gained from that adventure. John had once admitted that he might have been swept up in the fever of the Lewis and Clark bicentennial celebration and that his love for history and for all things to do with nature and outdoor exploring led him to do it – writing his book was a way to share the incredible knowledge and joy he gained from the journey. In *Tarzan the Mountain Man & The Pete King Fire of 1934*, John told the story of Ernie Bohn, who was the 1934 Otter Butte Lookout who basically built the 30 foot tower at Otter Butte by himself. Ernie's stories and journals may have helped nudge John into finally writing this memoir. *Above it All* is different than his previous books, though. In this book, John recounts his decades-long time on several different lookouts and it includes original personal and Forest Service journal notes from those years.

The stories and journal notes within these pages are a truly insightful look at the mostly solitary life of a lookout, the job required of the person who must be the eyes of the forest and the beacon for the firefighters, and also tells the story of who John is as a human being.

In his stories, he takes us on each experience, some of which are quite intense. For example, in his inaugural year as a lookout, John and his new bride and their cat had to make their way up to their mountaintop home by helicopter! Some of his experiences include living through a fire that he originally spotted, and in two weeks' time, had to be evacuated from the lookout. During a lull in the fire activity, John returned to the lookout to help fire wrap the tower to protect it, hoping that the tower would survive! As he vividly explains how it feels to stand on the porch of an over 40-foot tower and look out over the expansive and utterly breathtaking views of mountains that span three states, you might feel like you can actually see those vistas. How it feels and looks to sleep in an all-glass home, with the stars so close and vivid it's as if you could reach out and touch them... or how the animals of the mountaintop live and play, and sometimes become like friends. There's also the day to day living of a lookout, learning how (and how not to) try and take a warm bath in a wash tub, lightning striking the tower, picking huckleberries and making huckleberry pancakes.

There's so much that I could ramble on about in trying to share this book, but it is perhaps best to leave it to the reader to enjoy. The austerity of living, possibly so simple it's worthy of envy. What touched me the most about this memoir, and one thing that I do hope each reader will also take away from it, is that deeply imbued within these pages is not only the story of a genuinely great man, but also a love story. A love story for his wife, for nature, and the love and desire to live each day as an absolute adventure.

I hope you will all enjoy this book as much as I did – it is hard to walk away without a sense of reverence and appreciation for the fire lookouts, but maybe you also will be compelled to become a fire lookout, or visit the towers perched atop the mountains almost touching the sky, to span the view of state-to-state breathtaking mountain peak views, to smell those colorful phlox, spot a smoke, swim in a mountain lake, feed gray-jays from your hand – to be the one up above it all.

Thank you John for such a wonderful read!

Rachel Louise Burk

Stevensville, Montana

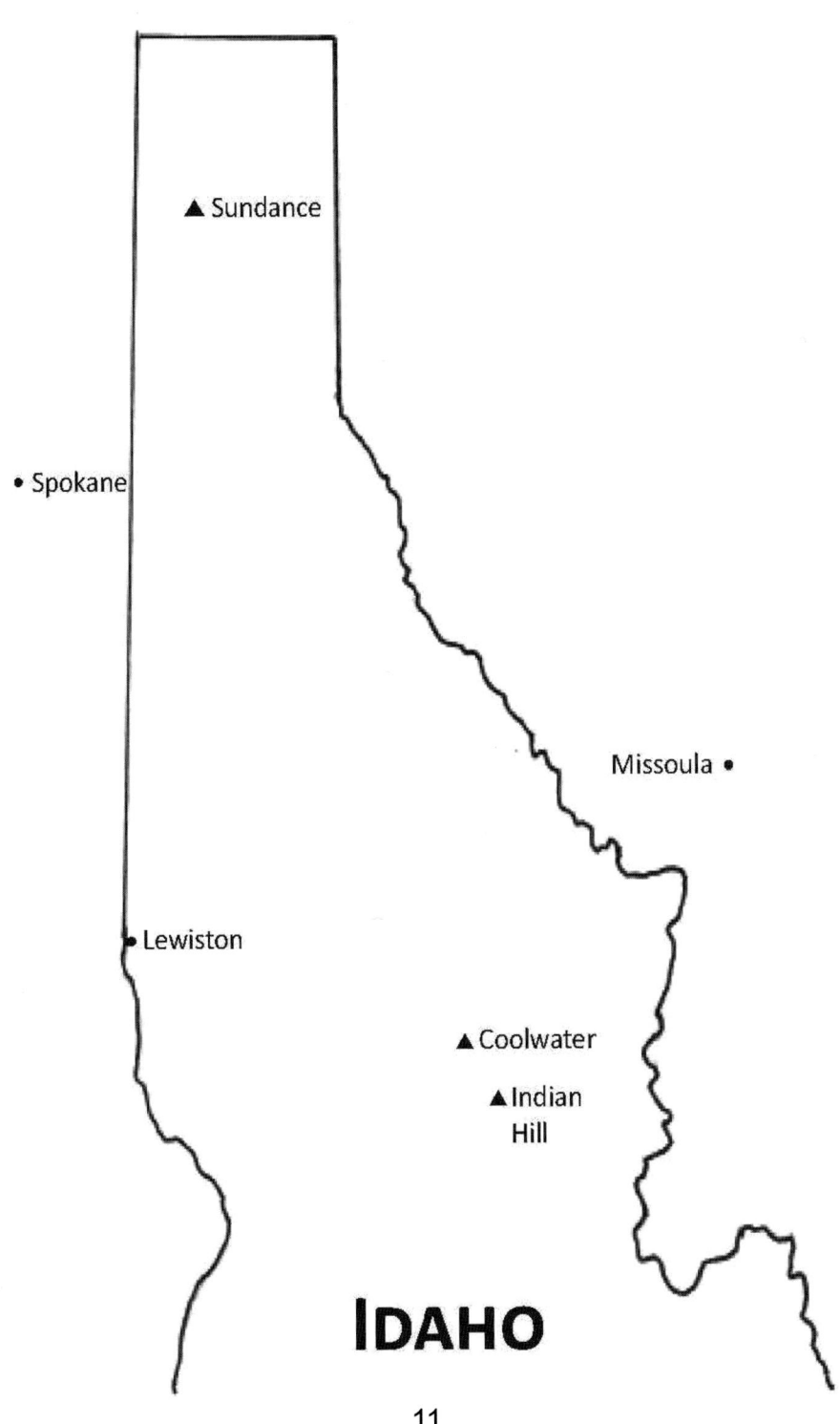

The First Year

June 22nd, 1974

    Like a gigantic prehistoric bird, the M.A.S.H.-type helicopter came in for a landing to the Fenn Ranger Station helipad over the serene Selway River, ready to carry us off to our new mountaintop home in the middle of the Idaho wilderness. Fresh from the big cities of Milwaukee and Denver, Judy, my bride of less than a year, our cat, Fritz, and I were about to be sent off to Indian Hill Lookout to spend the next four months probing the north-central Idaho mountains for wildfires. It was like Christmas morning for me, about to fulfill a dream of living in the wilderness like the Swiss Family Robinson on a 40-foot firetower.

    I didn't want to show my fear to Judy of riding in the ancient looking, old Korean-war-era helicopter that set down fifty feet from our pioneering family, the rotor wash blowing a mini hurricane into us. It didn't look safe. Heck, why weren't we going up to our mountaintop home in a spanky new Jet Ranger instead of this older-than-the-hills copter! But we didn't have a choice. All our supplies for the next four months were boxed up, weighed, and piled at our feet. With the engine shut down, the pilot and Wick loaded half our boxes into the baskets.

    Judy held onto our bobcat-looking cat with a vice grip, as Wick, our new boss, asked, "You ready, Crawford?"

    "You bet!" I eagerly answered.

    Wick gave us instructions on helicopter safety, and the plans of bringing up our remaining gear with him on the next flight. "How do you plan on carrying that cat?" he asked.

"In a pillowcase!" I replied, hoping like heck that it would hold him.

"Okay, well remember to always leave and approach the helicopter from the front...and by all means—keep your heads down!" Wick adamantly added.

"Will do!"

Then came the moment of truth. Wick escorted us around the front of the bubble-shaped copter, with our heads down, and we climbed inside...me wedged in the middle between the pilot, Friendsdorf, and Judy who held the pillowcase-wrapped Fritz tight on her lap.

"Have a good flight!" Wick said as he closed the door, sealing us inside the cramped quarters.

Friendsdorf, an ex-Vietnam pilot, flicked some switches, and the whir of the engine instantly sent our confined cat to seek his freedom, as he easily ripped his way out of the pillowcase and bolted out the door that the pilot opened. Friendsdorf cut the ignition, while Judy and I quickly got out in search of our little buddy.

"He's in the ranger station!" Wick exclaimed, sounding upset.

Judy and I scurried for the historic station two-hundred feet away, and were met by Ardys Taylor, the receptionist, and Forrest Hayes, the Assistant Ranger, at the front door, declaring that our cat shot down the stairs into the basement.

Judy and I found our little furry companion hiding in the break room, under a chair, shaking like a leaf.

"Maybe this will work a little better," Forrest said, handing me a cardboard box for Fritz.

"Thanks a bunch!" I replied, reaching under the chairs to get our cat against his will. I yanked him out, his claws scratching the cold, hard concrete floor like fingernails on a chalkboard.

We left the ranger station to try our second attempt at our inaugural flight to get to our new wilderness home.

Once again we were wedged inside the helicopter, with Judy holding Fritz in the cardboard box that sounded like a popcorn popper with our little buddy banging into the four walls.

Friendsdorf leaned towards me and announced very seriously…"If that cat gets out of that box while we're in the air, he's going for a flight without a parachute!"

Judy, hearing this stern warning, kept her arms over the top of the box to make sure Fritz wouldn't be dropping thousands of feet to his death.

Excited as heck to start our new life, but scared to death to fly in this old contraption, we watched as the pilot flicked some switches again and the engine started back up, the rotors whirling over our heads. This was it. I said a little prayer to make it safely to Indian Hill, and we took off, leaving the deep river valley, heading for the high mountaintop somewhere off to our east. Fenn Ranger Station soon appeared like a miniature train village, melting into the distance. The Selway River wound like a huge slithering snake far beneath our feet. Steep forested mountainsides rose out of the winding river canyon as the copter struggled to gain altitude.

It wasn't until we flew over a high ridge, and I could see the silvery tongue of Meadow Creek thousands of feet beneath my feet that my fear of heights started to get to me. I glanced at the instrument panel and saw that we were at 5,600 feet and still climbing towards the high ridge that rose above us to our east, the stick-model of a firetower finally starting to appear. Excitement of starting a new wilderness life squelched any residual fear of falling out of the sky, as we made our final approach to our new mountaintop address. Friendsdorf zoomed past to the south of the tower and banked hard to bring us into the wind. Expertly, he landed just behind a log cabin that sat nestled next to the shuttered tower.

The engine winding down to an idle, the pilot got out and opened our door, reminding us to keep our heads down when we left the copter. Judy got out first with the Fritz box, going to the other side of the cabin, away from the whirling copter's rotors.

After Friendsdorf and I unloaded the boxes onto the porch, he got back inside the bubble-shaped ship, revved the engine back up and lifted off for Fenn Ranger Station, soon becoming just a small speck in the western horizon.

First things first. Judy opened the flaps of the box and Fritz bolted out of his prison cell, immediately running up the path to the firetower that loomed above our heads a couple hundred feet away from the log cabin. We followed our little furry friend to check out our new home, up close and personal. Judy held Fritz at the base of the tower as I proceeded to climb the steep stairway, coming to a stop on the third landing, staring up at the catwalk gate that was another ten feet above my head. Taking in the bird's eye view from our new address, I saw the Selway River valley stretched for tens of miles off in the distance, ending in some high rugged mountains a good sixty miles off to our east. Then I took in the incredible scene to the north, gazing at an island of snow-covered mountains that lay beyond the deep Selway River valley below. Scanning the country to our west and south, I saw the Meadow Creek valley that we had just flown over. Huge snowbanks surrounded the tower, and blocked the road access, illustrating the reason why we were flown up.

I couldn't wait to officially become the new Indian Hill residents, and occupy our new home on stilts. But we had to patiently wait for our new boss to show up, which should be anytime now. Judy carried Fritz as we walked back down the lookout path to check out the incredible carpet of multi-colored wildflowers that covered the mountaintop between the snowbanks. I got down on all fours to smell the pink, purple and white phlox display, the alpine scent filling my senses.

Just like the lookout, we found the shuttered log cabin locked up tight. The sound of the helicopter in the distance broke the deep silence of the mountaintop, as we watched it make its approach. Judy held Fritz tight while the copter landed in a bed of phlox, its rotor-wash blowing another whirlwind into us. Friendsdorf killed the engine, as he and Wick got out to unload the wire baskets with the rest of our supplies. I helped them haul the boxes to the log cabin porch.

Getting back in the whirlybird, Friendsdorf took off for Fenn to bring up the propane that would run our stove and refrigerator for the summer, while Wick unlocked the log cabin door. He found a crow bar leaning against the wall and used it to pry open the two shutters, immediately ushering in light so we could check out the inside of the primitive cabin. With Judy catsitting outside, we untied the ropes that released the two mattresses that were hanging from the logs that formed the base of the loft. Putting them on the metal-framed beds, I did a quick survey of the 16x12-foot cabin. A large wood cookstove stood in the northwest corner, and a table was underneath the west window. A blue-painted wood hutch stood next to the stove on the north wall, and two bunks were on the south and east walls, with a small gray cupboard attached to the wall between them. An old caulk-worn ladder led to the loft.

"Give me a hand with this," Wick demanded, as we both lugged out the Indian Hill entrance sign that was leaning against the table. We carried it out to the sign support to the east of the cabin and hung it to officially become the Indian Hill Lookouts. "You ready to see your summer home?"

"I sure am, Wick!"

"Bring up one of those boxes with you, Crawford!"

"Will do!"

Wick grabbed the crow bar to loosen the lookout shutters, and I grabbed a box as we trudged up the narrow path between the cabin and the lookout tower, while Judy stayed with Fritz in a bed of colorful phlox. Totally out of breath in the high alpine air, I set the box down on the last tower landing, while my boss used his Forest Service key to unlock the trapdoor above our heads. Then Wick lifted the gate to our new home on stilts. I took the box through the catwalk to our living quarters forty feet above the Earth. I didn't admit my fear of heights to my boss as I looked down to see Judy and our little buddy on the ground. Yes, it definitely would take a bit to get used to being up this high. Wick pried open the door shutter, and again used his Forest Service key to gain entry into our humble abode. Holding the door shutter open, I carried in the box and set it on the green-tiled linoleum floor. I did a quick survey of our new house. A miniature-size refrigerator and stove stood on the east wall, with a small varnished-pine table on the south wall. The sill-height plywood bed sat along the west wall. And short, white-painted cabinets made up the rest of the east and west walls that were painted the color of the sky. A small mirror hung between two windows on the east wall.

"Let's bring some more of your gear up here while we're waiting for Friendsdorf to give us a hand with the shutters," Wick said. We won't be able to stay up here long after he returns. It's not safe to fly in the thin afternoon air."

I immediately felt a little nervous, wanting to pry as much information out of my new boss as possible before he left us all alone on the mountaintop for the next three to four months! The clock was ticking...I needed to get all my questions answered before he returned to civilization.

    After we hauled the rest of our summer's worth of supplies up the tall tower, Friendsdorf made his return, circling once over the lookout ridge and landing in the same spot, then shutting down. Then Friendsdorf, Wick and I struggled up the path with the two extremely heavy twenty-gallon propane bottles to the base of the lookout, and hooked them up to the copper tubing that came out of the ground by the timbered support. We climbed back up the steep stairs, and started to raise the shutters, "opening my eyes" for the summer. Facing my fear of heights, I couldn't help but look over the three-foot high railing as we lifted the shutters up to the overhead 2x4 framework supports, then used some nuts we found in the lookout to secure them ninety degrees from their resting positions. One after another, we struggled to get the eight shutters raised, with Wick telling me that it was my job to tighten the nuts with a crescent wrench after they left.

    The rest of the Crawford clan joined me as I took in the million dollar view. Mountains upon mountains were stacked up for as far as the eye could see...some maybe even a hundred miles away! I couldn't help but ask myself, "How in the world was I going to learn all these mountains, buttes, ridges, creeks and rivers?" Then there were more pressing issues...like where were we going to find our water source? We could use the snow for a while, but then what? Smack dab in the center of the 14x14-foot room was the Osborne Firefinder, which I learned about at Fire Guard School at Lookout Butte Lookout, but could certainly use a refresher course on how it worked. Then there was the large black box radio that Wick immediately hooked up to a 12-volt battery. We'd be a communication relay point for fire crews. And I didn't have a clue how to use it. The questions kept mounting in my head.

    Anxious to get off the mountain, Wick reviewed—a bit too

fast—the procedure on how to use the chest-high Osborne Firefinder, lining the peephole sight on Coolwater Lookout off to our northwest, then Anderson Butte Lookout to the southwest, and Vermilion Peak to our southeast. Pointing to the deep Meadow Creek Valley just to our west, my new boss said firmly, "Keep a close watch for any fires below you, because they could easily sweep over the mountain up here!" Advice I took to heart, as I didn't want us to be running for our lives from a raging forest fire this summer. He refreshed my memory of how to plot a fire on the 20-mile-radius circular map on the firefinder, going over townships, ranges, and sections. Wick also went over how to read the azimuth like using a giant compass. Then how to read the vertical scale that doubled as the peephole sight. He stressed for me to be sure to read the "Fireman's Handbook" to answer any more questions about finding and reporting forest fires. He showed me the fire detection forms, the lightning report forms and the false-smoke forms that were on clipboards in the firefinder cabinet.

Then he got down on all fours and lit the refrigerator so that we wouldn't lose any of the meat, fruit, and vegetables we had brought up. He showed us a cooler cabinet along the west wall that was screened-in through the floor. Lastly he lit the pilot light of the miniature-size stove before announcing, "Remember, Crawford...keep your eyes on all your country, but especially deep down in Meadow Creek!" With that Friendsdorf and Wick left our new lookout home, and got back in the waiting ship, taking off for Fenn. Judy and I waved from the catwalk as they soon disappeared from view, leaving us totally alone on the mountaintop, isolated from the rest of civilization.

The past couple weeks had been a whirlwind of activity in our lives, from our fast trip back to Milwaukee to get the station wagon that my parents sold us dirt cheap. Then it was the long trip back to Idaho, a week stay at the historic O'Hara house, while I attended Guard School and fought a fire, a huge shopping trip to Kooskia, and weighing all our boxes of supplies. And then the harrowing flight to our new summer home.

The lookout floor and bed were covered with our supplies that would get us through the next three to four months living up here...parkas that would get us through the snowstorms that we heard would hit the mountaintop almost every month, books to while away the time between fire checks, canned fruit and vegetables, lots of peanut butter, rice, beans, noodles, sugar, flour, pancake mix and syrup, cereal, powdered milk, Tang, bacon, eggs, crackers, bread, cheese, butter, and an assortment of meat to jam into the small freezer box. It was smaller than small, much too tiny to fit all the meat we had brought. We'd have to keep some in the refrigerator to use right away. We broke into the box with the perishables, and Judy first handed me the hamburger to stuff into the freezer. The pork chops and chicken I put into the still very warm refrigerator. What we couldn't fit in, we put into the air-cooled cabinet that Wick had showed us. Once the perishables were cooling, we did what we would be doing all summer long... took in the incredible view from out on the three-foot-wide catwalk. We closed the 2x6 gate to keep Fritz from escaping, as we soaked up the mind-blowing scenery.

Again, the snow-covered, high and rugged island mountain range across the Selway canyon to the north caught our attention, immediately becoming my favorite part of the huge 360-degree view. We cast our sights far off to the east, following the snaking Selway River canyon until it ended in a wall of granite half the state of Idaho away. Just off the lookout ridge to our east we could hear the sound of snowmelt cascading off the rock into the deep valley, which eventually led to another deep valley that led to the Selway River, a good five thousand feet beneath our feet. Off to the southeast, maybe fifteen miles away as the crow flies, stood some more high granite spires, with names yet unknown. The Indian Hill ridge was thickly covered with sub-alpine firs and lodgepole pines, which blocked much of our view to the south. Anderson Butte Lookout, which Wick had pointed out, stood tall on a prominent mountaintop ten miles to the southwest. On our horizon to the southwest stood another snow-covered nameless mountain range. Fifty miles or so beyond the mountains directly to the west, lay a huge patchwork quilt of wheat and canola fields of the Camas Prairie that Judy and I had seen close up when we came through on our trip from Denver in late May on a mission to find a forestry job. We looked out to the northwest, on Coolwater Lookout, Mark and Cindy Pfau's summer home, a shorter-tower than Indian Hill, sitting on a sharp rocky point a good fifteen air miles away. Fritz, obviously unafraid of the forty-foot height above the rocky knob that the tower sat on, jumped up on the short 2x4 railing, doing a tightrope walk around the catwalk, scaring the heck out of us as he too checked out his new surroundings. Judy grabbed our little buddy before he ended up falling forty feet down to the ground.

Off to the south of the tower, past the log cabin, we could see the obvious path to the outhouse at the edge of the five-acre clearing. The path to our spring, though, I couldn't see, so we'd have to depend on the snow that covered a lot of the mountaintop for our water needs. "I'm going to get some snow so we can melt it on the stove," I announced to Judy, who was digging into the boxes for our clothes, books, canned goods, and dry goods to shove into the drawers and cabinets that lay strategically below our four glass walls of four-pane windows.

"I'll keep Fritz up here while you're gone."

"Good idea."

I grabbed the large enameled dish pan from the counter next to the stove, and headed out the door on a mission to supply my family with a bunch of snow to melt for drinking, cooking, and washing dishes and ourselves. I creaked open the closed catwalk gate and secured it with a hook onto a large eye-bolt attached to the lookout. Down the steep four flights of stairs, I got to the boardwalk and made my way down the footpath to the log cabin, where I hoped to find a shovel. Bingo. A fire pack with a shovel was hanging on the inside east wall. I untied it from the fire pack, and took it out to the first large snowbank, which was a good five feet deep, extending for about forty feet just to the west of the cabin. I dug into the old snowdrift, and got to the cleaner snow underneath, and filled the pan with a mound of snow, hoping it would supply our needs for the rest of the day. When I went to return the shovel to the cabin, I couldn't help but explore a little bit more, and opened the drawer of the cabinet that hung from the south wall. Out jumped a mouse, scaring the living tar out of me! I had disturbed the cabin resident who had a huge nest in the drawer. With my nerves settling just a bit, I climbed the caulk-worn ladder to check out the loft. Upstairs I saw a pile of lumber, waterbags hanging from the log purlins, and a canvas army cot. I took the broom from the corner and swept up all the mouse turds of the mouse house.

  Next stop...the outhouse that I had seen from the firetower. I wandered down the path, past the helispot, to the edge of the woods where we'd have to hike to get to our new bathroom. It was a smelly, rickety affair, leaning over a bit, but thankfully still standing. I checked inside and found a mouse-shredded roll of toilet paper. Luckily I had remembered to bring some with our supplies. When I walked back up the outhouse path, I saw a lonely sight...a flagpole just off the lookout path without its flag. I opened the screen door and checked in the drawer below the mouse-nest one and found the stars and stripes. Carrying the wash basin of snow and the flag, I made my way to the base of the twenty-foot, white-painted pole and attached the red, white and blue and raised what completed our new lookout home at the edge of the

Selway Bitterroot Wilderness. As the flag flapped in the slight breeze, I noticed a large hawk doing circles above the tower, gaining altitude with each passing arc. Mesmerized by the bird of prey, I watched it until it got to be a mere speck high above me. Then I continued on, carrying our water supply up the four flights of tower steps.

"You look like you've been busy!" A pile of empty boxes were stacked along our north glass wall.

"I wonder how much water that will make?"

"Not sure," I replied, setting it on the burner of the miniature stove. "First things first!"

"What's first?" my wife asked, filling the cabinet between the stove and the refrigerator with the canned goods we brought.

"We can use that Tang we brought up here to make some slushes!"

"Tang is not my favorite, but I'll give it a try."

Judy handed me the jar of powdered orange sweetener from the cabinet. Then I got some glasses out of the drawer. Grabbing a spoon from the kitchen table drawer, I scooped out some snow into the plastic glasses and proceeded to make a couple of slushes. "Enjoy!" I handed Judy a glass of snow-filled delight. "Here's to a great summer on Indian Hill!" We touched glasses.

We both slurped up the lookout slushes, enjoying them like little kids at the Wisconsin State Fair. Then I lit the stove to start the process of getting serious about melting the huge mound of snow in the wash basin. I watched in amazement and much dismay at what I had hoped would be enough water to last the rest of the day melt away to about a quarter of the size of the original mound of snow. Pouring the water into a large pot we found in the cupboard, I made another trip to the ground, shoveling more snow into the large enameled basin.

    After Judy finished unpacking all the boxes and bags, the bed was next. Conveniently, the last lookout resident had piled a bunch of sheets and bedding on the thin mattress, which we used to really make our house a home. A couple of pillows that we found in the lookout attic completed our sleeping nook that was quite small in size. We definitely wouldn't have much room to toss and turn in the night.

    Doing household chores almost blinded me to the fact that I was up here for one sole purpose...to be a fire spotter! I was definitely not doing my job. I gazed out over the mountains, taking in the incredible scene again to see if I could find a smoke drifting out of the endless wrinkled carpet of green. Within twenty minutes I could tell that all was quiet, and went in search of some maps that would help me figure out my seen area. Bingo! The map that I was searching for sat right smack dab in the middle of the room...the Osborne Firefinder. I grabbed the handle of the firefinder and immediately directed it at the highest point in my new favorite mountain range to the north of the Selway River. I stared through the brass peephole sight, and aimed it like a gun, using the cross-hairs at the opposite end to line up what I quickly found out was Fenn Mountain, in the middle of the Selway Crags. The country that I knew would take me weeks to learn, I would do little by little. Right now, though, besides the Crags, I wanted to learn the creeks just off the lookout ridge to my east. Bluff Creek, with its bluffs lining the west side of the elevated valley, was a place I knew I would like to explore some day. Mica Creek lay just to the east of Bluff, with Berry Creek a little further east. Those drainages flowed north deep into Otter Creek. Satisfied that I at least knew some of my country, I took another quick scan over the rest of my area for fires, then grabbed the Fireman's Handbook to go over the "detection section" that Wick told me to read.

Between fire lookouts, and reading in the Fire manual, I went on another snow-gathering mission, bringing a roll of toilet paper for the outhouse. On the ground, I couldn't help but get down on all fours and smell the sweet alpine aroma of the colorful phlox again. Our lives have become very simple now, with our one and only mission...to discover all forest fires before they could become raging infernos! Totally immersed in nature in the Idaho wilderness, we'd take in the hawk shows, elk grazing along the ridge, deer, and maybe even a bear or cougar stealthily making its way below us. And then there were the thunderstorms that would produce the lightning that we were told would start most of the forest fires we'd spot. Anticipation brewed inside me as I looked forward to everything about this new lookout way of life.

Day 2 0200 hours

Flap...bang...bang...bang! Flap...bang...bang...bang! I woke from the middle of a good dream, suddenly realizing that something was seriously wrong with the lookout! Huge wind gusts from out of the west were buffeting the mountaintop, causing the shutters to flap like a huge bird's wings, quickly reminding me of what I had forgotten to do—tighten the shutters like Wick had instructed me to do before he left. Judy woke up too, shouting in the pitch black, "What the heck is making all that noise?"

"It's the shutters banging up and down on the nuts!"

"What can you do about it?" She sounded as concerned as I was.

"I'm not about to go out there and tighten them in the dark!" I cringed at the thought of the nuts working their way to the ends of the bolts and the shutters crashing into the windows. I discreetly kept those dire thoughts to myself.

"Great way to spend our first night on lookout!" Judy added sarcastically. Fritz joined the chorus, meowing loudly as he pranced over our legs on the cold, hard bed.

"I'll deal with it in the morning. Try to go back to sleep!"

Thankfully the windstorm was fairly short-lived. After a half an hour the shutters stopped banging and the tower stopped shaking, finally allowing us to go back to sleep.

0800 hours

I did get up at around 0600 hours and tightened the shutters with the crescent wrench I found in the west-wall cabinet. Now we were ready for the next wind event.

The radio came alive with the Horse Creek research station calling over the radio, "Indian Hill, this is Roberts."

I grabbed the hand-held mike to my mouth, talking on the Forest Service radio for the first time, "Roberts, this is Indian Hill...go ahead."

"Give me a 4-5!" he announced across the airwaves, his voice booming in the lookout like he was right next door.

4-5...4-5. I quickly looked at the four-code messages posted on the firefinder and found out that it meant he wanted me to switch over to automatic repeat, saving me from embarrassing myself with relaying the wrong message. Easy peasy. Just switch the toggle switch on the radio to automatic repeat and voila...let the fancy communication device do all the work. "Indian Hill on 4-5," I relayed to Roberts.

Now all I had to do is wait until he called for a 4-6 (off repeat). I listened for the magic words for minutes, much longer than I expected. Surely he would call anytime now! But still no 4-6 came across the airwaves. What the heck was going on?

When I finally switched it off repeat, the very agitated voice of Bob Wickersham **boomed** into the lookout…"Indian Hill, what the hell are you doing up there…sleeping?"

I cringed at Wick's cussing me out that shook me to my core! Figuring that responding to my boss certainly wasn't going to help the situation, I asked Judy, "Did you hear Roberts call for a 4-6?"

"Didn't hear a word after he asked for the 4-5!"

"Yeah…I didn't hear anything either!"

"Just try not to let Wick get to you."

"I'll try." Totally unnerved from getting yelled at over the radio, I couldn't help but think of how embarrassing it was to totally screw up my first official duty as a lookout. I figured that Roberts just forgot to call for me to go off repeat. There just wasn't any other explanation.

I spent the rest of the day keeping busy, and trying to erase the 4-5 fiasco from my memory, which wasn't working too well. Continuing to supplement our water supply I carried pan after pan of snow up the tower steps, doing fire lookouts at least every 20 minutes, and even scraping some paint on the lookout. And thank God, there were no more requests for a 4-5 the rest of the day.

🐝 Day 7 1030 hours

Our days were becoming more attuned with nature as our lookout season wore on…keeping track of the elk and deer residents, the eagles, hawks, ravens, and turkey buzzards that soared above the ridge, the incredible sunrises over Montana and the equally beautiful sunsets over Oregon! Every day I kept up my mission to learn the country before me…the ridges, buttes, mountains, creeks and rivers finally getting names, working out from the closest geographical features first. I kept up a vigil for forest fires, not wanting to miss a fire that could make the green forest black. Judy and I continued peeling paint, something that became therapeutic. And I finally learned the location of the spring from an old map that I found in the hutch in the log cabin. Giving up on getting snow from the dwindling snowbanks, I discovered the trail that led to two springs…one on the road about a mile from the lookout, complete with a horse trough, and another smaller one a couple hundred yards above the lower one, a private secret cove of a water source that probably only past lookouts knew about. Instead of carrying snow up to the lookout, now I was carrying a leaking-like-a-sieve five-gallon firefighting trombone pump water bag on my back, along with a couple of canteens around my neck up the trail every other morning. Everything was going along great on the mountain, despite the 4-5 mess up, and even that problem was solved, with me finding out from the radio handbook that when Roberts asked for the automatic repeat, I only flicked one switch when I needed to flick two, which would have allowed me to hear the conversation. Never again would I mess that up.

Suddenly the Forestry radio came alive with the familiar-sounding voice of Bob Wickersham. "Indian Hill, this is Fenn," he announced.

I came inside from the catwalk after doing another fire check, picking up the mike and replying, "Fenn, this is Indian Hill."

"Somebody has reported seeing a smoke in your area. Take a good look around and get back to us if you spot anything."

"Will do, Wick," I nervously responded. Immediately I looked out and saw this huge black column of smoke coming from across Meadow Creek that I had obviously missed! Shaking like a leaf, I quickly zero'd the firefinder in on the base of the smoke, and got out my fire detection report forms. Okay...now try to stay calm and figure out a legal on it, I told myself. I plotted the column on the map right at Fall's Point. Jittery, I wrote down the location by landmarks on the form, the legal description, azimuth, vertical angle, size, rate of spread, wind speed, drift of smoke and aspect. Like giving a speech in my college speech class, I nervously called in my first fire report from Indian Hill.

"That legal is not right!" Wick coldly announced. "Check your firefinder again and call me back with the right legal!"

I couldn't believe my ears! I was certain I was correct on my legal, as it was coming from a known point on the map at Fall's Point.

Again the radio came alive, this time with the calm voice of Rhondy Lyons, a member of the fire crew. "Fenn this is Lyons."

"Lyons, go ahead," Wick responded.

"Indian Hill does have the right legal."

"10-4."

"Lyons clear."

It was a small victory to have the location correct. But why hadn't I seen that obvious as heck black column sooner? I had been on a fire watch that I did according to the Fireman's Handbook's instructions to zig zag through each major drainage to thoroughly look for fires. I had been zigging and zagging through the drainages on the east side of the lookout when that fire was blazing on my west side, undetected from my prying eyes in the sky. I had learned a valuable lesson from missing this obvious practice fire...stop doing long staredowns with the drainages, and look more generally over all my country. If I see something suspicious, look through binoculars to check it out. Giving up on what the Fireman's Handbook prescribed, I was learning on my own what worked and what didn't as a fire lookout. But no matter that I was merely doing what the book described, didn't erase the fact that Wick had two strikes against me...the 4-5, and now the practice-fire blunder. I couldn't get a third, or I knew I would be looking for a different job. One good thing in my favor, though, was the legal description that I gave was correct.

🐝 July 4th

It wasn't like we wanted to leave the lookout even for a day, but all the forces were lined up to allow us to get our rig from down at the ranger station. Except for a few patches of snow, the road was mostly clear, and Wick had the campground recreation assistant driving up to bring us down to civilization.

Since the road was closed because of all the snow, we hadn't heard the foreign sound of a rig grinding up it till now. Our chauffeur, Don Baty, was coming to get us. I learned to love the isolation from society that the snow had brought us. No cars, pickups, trail bikes, or three-wheelers for the first couple of weeks had given us so much peace and quiet. For miles, we heard the Forest Service pickup get closer to our summer home. Louder and louder it got, the engine noise canceling out the sound of the wind, and the cry of the hawk we saw circling above the ridge. The first signs of civilization since the day we arrived, came barreling around the last bend in the road too quickly, interrupting our peace and quiet.

Like two birds taken from their nest, Judy and I left the lookout and went on a fast and furious two-hour journey down to the ranger station which we left two weeks ago. Don, the first person we'd seen since Wick and Friendsdorf left the lookout, was a fast driver, speeding past the Copper Butte Trailhead, the spring that I went to almost every day now, a small 10-foot waterfall just beyond a meadowy hillside I knew

I'd have to check out, rounding bend after bend, getting me dizzy. Hoping that we wouldn't meet head on with an uphill driver, we thankfully made it to the bottom of the road in one piece, at Slim's Campground, where we saw all the sites filled with campers. The rest of the journey to get our station wagon was a blur, as we barreled along the Meadow Creek Road, then the Selway River Road that led us back to Fenn Ranger Station.

With Wick taking the 4th off, and the grocery store in Kooskia closed for the holiday, we hopped in our station wagon and began the long drive back to our mountaintop home. Taking it at a much more sane pace, we noticed all that we had missed on the fast and furious trip down...all the hidden-away campgrounds on the Selway, the sandbars along the beautiful emerald-green river, the huge cedar and ponderosa pine trees, the osprey nests, the trailheads that led up to Coolwater Ridge, the Selway Falls cabin, and the pristine Meadow Creek drainage. Then the even slower drive back up the extremely steep Indian Hill road from Slim's Camp, keeping the Pontiac station wagon in low range. The abrupt drop-off to Meadow Creek for the first mile, then the Selway far below the road, scared the living heck out of us, as I made sure not to get too close to the edge. Switchback after switchback, we crept up the mountain road, closing in on the tower at 6,810 feet. Getting to the small waterfall we had seen earlier, I stopped so we could check it out and fill the canteens that I had brought along. Getting wet to get a drink, we absorbed the beauty of the Little Creek mini-falls.

It was when I reached into the lookout attic to get some more Tender Vittles for Fritz and some canned peaches for supper, that I noticed a treasure trove of cast aside items— logbooks from past lookouts—Joyce Wallinder, John and Donna Moody, the Baldwins, and Chip Foley. Standing on the wobbly glass-insulated lightning stool, I paged through Joyce's

1973 journal, reading about Al Maynard, the District Packer, helping her move in last year. Then I checked out Chip's 1965 diary, reading about him digging post holes—one a day—for the corral by the outhouse. I surveyed other lookout items... an egg beater, a spatula, a large cast-iron frying pan, some old firefinder alidade maps, some plastic wash basins, old Forest Service Kapok sleeping bags, extra sheets, and what really caught my eye...a collapsible canvas shower bucket with a wide showerhead on it.

"Judy...you won't believe what I found up here!"

"What's that?" she responded, working away making a spaghetti dinner.

"A shower bucket!"

"You're kidding! A shower sounds wonderful!"

I grabbed the green canvas bucket, and stepped off the lightning stool. "Look at this!"

"Amazing you haven't seen it up there till now!"

"Yeah, no kidding."

"Do I have a date?"

"For what?"

"A shower early in the morning if the wind's not blowing. We'll take turns out on the east-side catwalk."

In a flash our little buddy jumped up on the lightning stool and leaped into the attic, his front paws making it, but his back paws struggling to gain entry. Leaving paw marks on the ceiling, he finally got up there, stretched out and used the 2x4 roof support for a scratching block.

🐝 *Early on July 5th*

Everything was set for our inaugural lookout shower… little to no wind, a conveniently placed nail on the northeast shutter for the bucket, a beach towel draped over the railing, a soap dish and wash cloth on the window ledge, and a large porcelain wash basin with very warm water in it.

"You ready?" I asked my wife.

"Ready as I'll ever be!" she said. "Hold the towel if the wind comes up!"

"Will do!" I got out the oak captain's chair and put it underneath the shutter. Then I made sure the showerhead was turned to the closed position before dumping three gallons of steaming water into it. "You hold the bucket while I pour."

"O.K."

I lifted the heavy canvas bucket, stood on the chair and hooked it over the nail. "Ready for some nice hot water streaming all over your body?"

"Let's hope that the wind doesn't come up!"

I moved the chair out of the way and screwed the showerhead counterclockwise, with beads of steaming water cascading off Judy's body. A short rinse was followed with her soaping up a few feet away while I took my turn under the lookout shower. Then I stood aside and lathered up, letting Judy rinse off.

"Ahh…that feels great!" she exclaimed.

All soaped up, unable to see, I waited patiently until Judy finished. "It's all yours!"

I snuck in, the warm water streaming off my body, as I gazed out over the expansive wilderness. Much too soon the shower was over and I grabbed Judy's towel to dry off in the warm sunshine.

We followed up our wonderful lookout shower with a scrumptious pancake breakfast at the knotty pine kitchen table, overlooking hundreds of thousands of acres of the wrinkled carpet of green to the Salmon River Breaks far off in the distance to our south. Then we washed the dishes, the plumbing being one big toss of the dishwater over the railing, waterfalling down off the rock outcrops just to the north of the lookout.

Life at Indian Hill settled into a routine...waking up super early with the sun shining into our all-glass house, then leaving on a waterhaul (occasionally I'd use the station wagon) on the spring trail with Fritz who learned how to hike with me, checking in to Fenn Dispatch at 0800, 1200, and 1600 hours, doing fire observations three times an hour, going over more of my country with the topographic maps and the Osborne Firefinder, learning the false smokes in my area—the Elk City Mill, the snowbanks and clearings that looked suspiciously like smoke, and reading in one of the many books we brought along to fill in the time. Now we were also starting to see a trickle of visitors coming up to see a real fire lookout. It took a little while for us to get adjusted to them invading our space. I pretty much adjusted, but Judy didn't, hoping like heck that I wouldn't invite them into our living quarters from out on the catwalk. Then there were the after-hours hikes we'd do from the tower...going out to the huge wildflower-filled meadowy hillside we had seen from the road, checking out the top of the bluffs that towered over Bluff Creek that was in sight of the tower, hiking to what I called the patrol point that was on the old Trail #621 to Otter Butte, and then continuing on to the highest point on the Indian Hill Ridge. We also checked out the Copper Butte Trail that led into the Selway Bitterroot Wilderness, which started about a mile from the lookout. In the evenings, Judy and I sat around the radio for the Breeze Session, something we rarely missed. From 1930 to 2030 lookouts traded notes with other lookouts, talking about fires they reported, what they baked in their lookout ovens, even playing Chess over the airwaves. It was a time I could talk to Mary Jo on Anderson Butte, and Mark and Cindy on Coolwater. Shortly after an amazing sunset we'd go to bed, with Fritz tucked away in a little kapok sleeping bag tent we'd make for him on the captain's chair. With millions of sparkling diamonds of stars overhead, we'd slowly fall off to sleep to dream of more wonderful days on Indian Hill.

July 9th

Something was different about today. I had seen pictures of early-morning storm-indicator clouds—altocumulus castellates—posted on side of the firefinder table, and this morning I was indeed seeing them above the lookout ridge. I had been preparing for this day ever since I arrived, with my lightning strike and fire report forms ready—going over instructions on what to do if a storm is imminent...close the door and all windows, turn off the radio and unplug the antennae. And last but certainly not least...get on the lightning stools and stay away from all metal objects!

I didn't want to admit this to Judy, as I stared out at the castellates clouds from the catwalk, but the thought of being in a lightning storm on the highest point around kind of unnerved me. Surely the tower could get struck and we'd only have these glass-insulated stools to protect us. I tried to not show my concern to Judy, who was inside working on a needlepoint project.

Nerves led to more old cancerous paint getting scraped off the lookout. My other half joined me, also working on scraping the white-painted building. "Looks like we might be in for something," she said, staring up the clouds.

"If that cloud chart's right, it sure does look like we'll get a storm later on," I added, showing her a five-inch paint strip I'd just peeled off.

"Nice job!" Judy exclaimed. "Got your lightning strike forms ready?"

"Ready as I'll ever be!"

We were settled into our afternoon routine, sitting out on the wind-shadowed south side of the lookout, soaking up the sunshine and taking in the million-dollar view, when I heard a panicked voice shoot across the airwaves…"Riggins, this is Dry Diggins!"

Quickly I slipped inside the lookout to hear the lookout's transmission better.

"Dry Diggins, this is Riggins."

"I've got lightning on the District going down up in the Seven Devils!"

"10-4 Dry Diggins. I'm ready for any fire reports."

"Guess these castellates clouds are no hoax," Judy said as she walked in the door.

Our eyes had laser focus on our far southwestern horizon, in the direction of the Seven Devils, and saw the dark line of clouds close to a hundred miles away.

"So you know the drill if lightning's close by!"

"Yeah…get on these lightning stools and hope we don't get struck!"

"That's for sure!"

"I'll take the high stool," Judy insisted, staring at the barstool-like lightning stool.

"Sounds good to me," I said. "I'll take the shorter one. And remember to sit a ways away from the stove and firefinder!"

I went out on the catwalk and brought in both our captain's chairs. While Judy started working on her needlepoint again, I nervously looked over the firefinder map to relearn my country. Horse Creek, Fall's Creek, Little Boulder Creek, SOB Creek, Island Creek, O'Hara Creek, Swiftwater Creek, Fall's Point, SOB Ridge, Lookout Butte, Lodge Point, and Anderson Butte to the west of me. Bluff Creek, Mica Creek, Berry Creek, Birch Creek, Otter Creek, Buck Lake Creek, Highline Ridge, Otter Butte, Copper Butte, Little Copper Butte, and Wylies Peak off to our east. Then I went over the country to my north and south, feeling pretty satisfied that I had it all down.

Next I put graphite between the firefinder rings to get it to slide better, and checked the orientation on two prominent points; Coolwater Lookout at 316 degrees...check, and Vermilion Peak at 133 degrees 15 minutes...check.

I was ready...

One after another, fire lookouts were catching the brunt of the storm, as it marched its way east...Cold Springs, Graves Point, Chair Point, Slate Point, Sawyer Ridge, Corral Hill, and Pilot Knob. Pilot Knob was getting close...darn close. Thirty-miles close. The anvil-shaped, 30,000-foot-high cloud was heading our way as if we had a bull's eye on us! We could start to see lightning jab at the earth, Pilot Knob going 10-7 (out of service) for lightning. I went out on the west-side catwalk to see if I could hear any thunder. All was eerily quiet—no wind, no rumbles...the *calm* before the storm.

I couldn't help but reflect back on growing up in Wisconsin.

As a family we'd hide out in the basement for hours at a time as storms that bred tornados raged outside our home. Thankfully there were no tornados in the mountainous west, but I knew that the inch-thick steel cables that held the tower aloft were there for a good reason...to keep us from blowing over in these storms' high winds. And that's what I started feeling, as a westerly breeze started up. The storm was approaching...

I started to see more downstrikes jab at the mountainsides out by Pilot Knob Lookout, jotting down their locations on my lightning strike form. Newsome Creek was next to get hit with lightning, just to the east of Pilot Knob. Then Iron Mountain...a mere twenty miles to the west. Off in the distance I could finally hear the low rumble of thunder. The storm was coming our way. Then I saw another lightning strike go down on Iron Mountain, followed by a huge black-as-night smoke just south of it. Then another lightning strike jabbed at the earth, out by Hamby Saddle, starting another huge flare-up. I zero'd in on the smokes with my firefinder and wrote down their locations on my fire detection forms. But the fires that had started were quickly being snuffed out by the thick veil of rain that swept out of the massive cloud to our west.

I had a bird's eye view of Horse Creek, just across the Meadow Creek canyon. It was shaped like a tuning fork... two forks of the drainage almost perfectly identical. There the Forest Service had a research station where they were studying the effects that logging had on the two streams, with one being logged and the other left untouched. It was an extremely important drainage to the Forest Service, and they didn't want it burned up. But with lightning now hitting the head of those two drainages hard, I was afraid of just that. More flare-ups shot high into the air, before the curtain of moisture blocked us from seeing if they kept going.

"You going to call those fires in?" Judy asked urgently, moving her lightning stool away from the firefinder.

"I'll wait till the rain passes before I report them."

Judy shut the west-side cranked-out window and closed the door...getting ready for the inevitable.

The massive thunderhead moved closer to our vulnerable home on stilts, more downstrikes stabbing at the earth—Fall's Creek, Horse Ridge, SOB Ridge also getting hit, with more huge black columns of smoke shooting high into the sky! Then again, what God had started, quickly got snuffed out by the wall of rain streaming out of the gigantic cloud.

The storm sweeping across Meadow Creek just below us triggered us into action, as I quick got on the radio and excitedly announced, "Indian Hill going 10-7 for lightning!" Then I turned the radio off and unscrewed the antennae, and hopped on my foot-high lightning stool, while Judy sat on hers.

Suddenly a strong gust of wind slammed into the lookout, as we felt the tower lean over to the east from the fury out of the west. Fritz nervously paced the window sill above the bed, as one after another, more lightning strikes struck just below us, loud thunderous roars following each bolt. More huge gusts of wind rocked the tower as lightning now stabbed tree after tree around us...flames shooting high in the air. Then, thankfully, the rain swept across the mountain, and hopefully put them out.

Flash...Bang! Momentarily blinded, we felt the loud bang shake the tower!

"We just got hit!" Judy cried out.

"That's for sure!" I yelled back.

Rain streamed down our windows, making it hard to see out. Lightning striking the tower, blowing up trees and starting them on fire, the huge winds, a driving rain! What more could we take? Fritz jumped up on the firefinder, the last place he should be if we got struck again. I quickly grabbed him and threw him on the bed. The driving rain started leaking through the windows into the lookout, the kapok sleeping bag bedspread getting wet as well as the floor.

Then, when we thought the worst would soon be over, hail started striking the west windows in the 60...70 mile-per-hour winds! Huge hailstones, the size of golf balls, threatened to break every pane, the noise deafening.

"Those windows might break!" I yelled over the roar of the hail to my partner two feet away.

"No kidding!"

"Let's get under the mattress!" I practically screamed to be heard.

We both abandoned the lightning stools, and took refuge from the storm under the thin mattress. Snuggled up with my wife, I couldn't help but wonder what if the windows *did* break. I also wondered if we were protected from lightning on this plywood bed. But I was a whole heck of a lot more afraid of the hail right now than the lightning to leave our protective fortress.

I could still hear muffled thunderclaps embedded with the wind-driven hailstone barrage, as I hoped the storm would finally pass so I could start doing my job. Kneeling on the hard plywood bed, I thought that any minute we'd be hearing the crashing of glass spraying the lookout room.

Ten minutes of tense-filled moments and I finally heard what I wanted to hear...silence. No more hail, or wind. Just some distant thunder as the storm marched its way east past the lookout ridge. I snuck out on the wet floor and immediately plugged the antennae back in and turned on the radio.

"What a storm!" Judy exclaimed, echoing my feelings.

"Hey! Look out at Horse Creek. The whole drainage is on fire! White smokes are everywhere!"

I didn't wait for a response and quickly went to work to let Fenn know that their whole research project was about to go up in smoke! I grabbed the mike and was about ready to call Fenn Dispatch about the inferno, when Judy calmly grabbed me by the shoulders and pointed west.

"Those aren't fires!"

"What the heck are you talking about? They've got to be fires!" I insisted.

"You see those light-blue smokes coming out of the mountainsides?"

I gazed out of the still-intact glass and..."Oh yeah...guess you're right! Thanks for keeping me from making a complete fool of myself!"

Giving up on the white "smokes" (I later found out that they were called waterdogs), I got busy zeroing the firefinder on the "real" blue smokes that dotted the mountainsides. I counted ten smokes that I could see and prioritized them...Horse Creek was first of course. Then I'd work on the ones I could see on Horse Ridge and Five-Mile Creek, SOB Ridge, Iron Mountain and Fall's Creek. So far nothing was showing on the home front...apparently the rain and hail had put them out. I wrote down all the details of my "real" first Horse Creek fire, which was near the confluence of the Main Fork and the East Fork—close to the research cabin—the Horse Creek Hilton. Azimuth, vertical angle, location by landmarks, legal description, base of smoke seen?, size of smoke, color of smoke, position on slope, rate of spread. As I held the microphone to my mouth, ready to call in my smoke, I thought how I couldn't screw this up. I had to have the legal correct or Wick would surely fire me! But I had to hurry up...I had a good ten more fires to report. So I keyed the mike and nervously called in a 4-7 (four code for reporting a forest fire) and relayed the details of Smoke #1. Mission accomplished. I reported my first fire! Then the second, third and fourth Horse creek fires got a little easier with practice. By the time I was done I had reported a total of fourteen forest fires on the District...a regular fire bust.

With smokejumpers, helitak, and station fire crews responding to the fires, we crunched our way out on the catwalk to see if we could spot any smokes off the lookout. Two inches of hailstones covered the boardwalk as we looked out over the white mountaintop. Nothing showed.

"You hear a plane?" Judy asked as we soaked up the sunshine.

"Yeah, I sure do!" I looked to the west, again seeing my fires across Meadow Creek still smoking away. And then I had a visual. "It must be air patrol."

"Maybe he sees something tucked below us."

We heard it circling just off to our west, when air patrol checked in to Fenn Dispatch. We made our way back inside.

"Do you have a fire reported in Little Creek, just to the west of Indian Hill?"

"No, we don't have a report on that one," Gary Dutcher, the dispatcher, responded.

"Well, you got one just below the road down here. I'll paper the fire on the road just above the smoke."

"Sounds good."

He gave a legal description and cleared himself off the air.

"Judy, do you see anything down there?"

"No, not a thing."

"Me either. Well, it must be small, or way down below us if

neither one of us can see it."

We went back out on the catwalk to watch air patrol paper the fire. Round and round they went, then a roll of toilet paper got tossed out of the Cessna, the long stream slowly falling to the ground.

"Indian Hill, this is Fenn."

Quickly I made my way back inside the lookout. "Fenn, this is Indian Hill," I answered, a little out of breath.

"We want you to respond to that fire below you," Dutcher announced over the Forest radio. "Ready to copy the legal?"

"Ready to copy."

I copied the legal in my official logbook and cleared myself from the radio.

"You better be careful down there!" Judy insisted, going in the cupboard by the tiny refrigerator to get something. "I'll make you a couple sandwiches to take along."

"That would be great!" Soon I had two peanut butter sandwiches in hand and got ready to go off and fight a forest fire. "Don't worry about me. I'll be safe!"

"You better!"

Judy handed me the keys that I forgot as I gave her a quick kiss and headed out the door. Down the four flights of stairs, and down the lookout path to the log cabin I went to get the fire pack that was hanging on the wall. A Pulaski and shovel were lashed to the fire pack, along with a manty filled with Army C Rations and a headlamp. A canteen dangled from the frame of the pack. All of a sudden it really dawned on me. I was about to fight a forest fire all by myself! And not only that, but I was leaving my wife all alone on the firetower. Not that I was a complete novice at fighting a fire...I had that week of Fire Guard School at Fenn and I fought a 2-acre blaze on the western edge of the District before I came up here. I waved goodbye to Judy on the catwalk and drove to the spring and filled the canteen, then continued my way to where it looked like the plane was circling. Down the road I went, keeping my eyes peeled for smoke below the road and toilet paper hanging in the trees above the fire.

Past the meadowy hillside below the horse trough, beyond the Little Creek waterfall I went, scoping out the mountain below the road for the elusive smoke I had yet to see. Creeping down the road, now in the area where I saw the plane circling, I saw *something* that looked funny. Blue-gray amongst the emerald green of the hundred-foot tall cathedral of firs and spruces. Immediately I slammed on the brakes and got out of the station wagon. I zero'd in on the "different" color, and sure enough...a hundred yards below the road was a definite smoke! The aerial spotter was a good shot, as I looked up and saw the toilet paper waving in the slight westerly breeze, hung up in the branches of a stately Douglas Fir. I wolfed down a sandwich as I stared at the source of the smoke deep down the one hundred percent slope. Now I could make out flames. I better get down there, and fast! I strapped the fire pack over my shoulders, and grabbed the other sandwich and gallon canteen, and off I went to go put out the fire.

It was no walk in the park as I tripped over branches, stumbled over downed trees, and crashed through brush to get to the smoking, crackling forest fire. In five minutes I was there, ready to do what all firefighters do—dig a trench around it first. I untied the shovel and Pulaski from my fire pack and began digging a two-foot trench around the twenty by twenty-foot fire. Like a ground-digging badger, I dug a ditch a couple feet away from the two-foot-high flames. But the flames were spreading fast, so I started throwing nice cool, moist dirt at the active fire. Shovel full after shovel full got tossed, until most of the hot spots were cooled down. Then it was back to digging and chopping roots with the Pulaski and cleaning out the trench with the shovel. A strong westerly breeze made its way under the canopy and restarted what I thought were extinguished flames. Shovel full after shovel full of dirt got tossed again until the fire got snuffed out. I started digging the fire line with more urgency, skipping the chopping of roots part to hurry myself along. Within the hour the fire was finally contained and hopefully controlled. I grabbed the other sandwich and took five. The next job would be to mop it up, potato-patching everything inside the line. After I washed the sandwich down with some ice-cold spring water, I began the process of putting the fire to bed, without the trombone pump water bag that I didn't bring because it didn't have a connection hose. I was about halfway through mopping it up, when I thought I heard voices.

"Hey Indian Hill!" someone yelled from up on the road.

"I'm down here!" I immediately hollered back.

A few minutes later I saw Forrest Hayes and Johnny Smith appear between the trees.

"Hey, look Forrest...Crawford hasn't even left enough fire here to make a pot of coffee!" Johnny exclaimed.

"Good to see you guys! I haven't put it completely out yet."

"Well, you did a heck of a job, John!" Forrest added, making me swell with pride.

"It was flaming pretty good when I first got here," I commented. "But throwing dirt at it really helped a lot."

"We'll take over from here," Forrest said.

"Thanks a lot, you guys!"

I used the parachute cord to lash the tools back on my firepack, took a swig from the orange canteen and bid the two Fenn firefighters good-bye.

Life got back to normal after the huge storm, as we took morning and evening strolls amongst the wildflowers around our home on stilts...the colorful phlox fading away with the beautiful cream-colored beargrass replacing it. Then the yellow sulpherflower and purple penstemon and larkspur followed close behind. Clothes got washed with an old-fashioned washboard, and water got hauled up with a rope pulley to our living quarters. Fritz always went along with us as we checked out our lookout yard and beyond. Back to the meadow overlooking upper Meadow Creek we went, to the patrol point along the trail and then to the highest point on the Indian Hill ridge, a mile away.

On July 12th, on a day off, we left Fritz locked up in the lookout with a box of Tender Vittles if he got hungry. We knew that he could fend for himself as he had learned how to open his cat food box, pull out the packets of Vittles and tear open the packages. We topped off his Forest Service China water bowl with some spring water and took off on a hike into the wilderness to explore the Little Copper Butte area, eight miles east of the tower.

We hiked a mile on the road to the Otter Butte and Copper Butte Trailhead, marked Otter Butte 6 miles, and Copper Butte 4 miles. In a hundred feet, the two trails split, Trail #621 going straight up the ridge and the one we were taking, Trail #602, contouring around to the right. Our first stop, a quarter mile down the narrow path, was the beautiful wildflower-filled meadowy mountainside we had hiked to before. Beyond that it was all new country to both of us, as we started our descent to the saddle between Indian Hill and Copper Butte. Down and down we went, until we got to the saddle. Humungous firs and spruces created a canopy so thick it kept the sun from reaching the ground. Then we made a long, hard climb up to Copper Butte, three switchbacks later topping out on the ridge where we were greeted with a great view of the lookout tower in the distance. I took a picture, then we continued on, going on the backside of Copper Butte, coming to a really neat old dead snag, which we dubbed the Grandfather Snag. I snapped another picture to record our find, then continued on to the Prospect Point Trail junction. Snow clung to the backside of the butte. Our goal...to get to another huge snowbank that we could see from Indian Hill, halfway between Little Copper Butte and Drake Saddle. Knowing we'd be pushing dark to check it out, we got a move on it, picking up the pace.

A strange scene met us when we were climbing up to the top of Little Copper Butte. A wide, beargrass-filled swath in the lodgepoles had been cut years ago, for what reason I didn't know. Lots of stumps lined the narrow path to the top of the butte.

It was a dramatic, Sound of Music type of scene as we made our way along the open ridge that formed the divide between Berry and Buck Lake Creeks. The Selway Crags stood majestic, across the Selway, their steep talus-sloped, snow-covered mountainsides centering the awesome view. Another mile of open ridgerunning and we finally arrived at the huge leftover snowdrifts that I had set my sights on since we arrived on Indian Hill. I had one thing on my mind...to do some skiing without the skis. Judy and I had a picnic lunch, gazing back to the west at our home that looked so tiny and lonely without its residents.

Lunch done, I put my plan into action...climbing to the top of the big drift. I took a running start, hooting and hollering like a little kid, and boot skied down the old snow, Judy capturing it on film. A half dozen more runs and I was done, glad to not have broken a leg.

On the way back we veered off the main trail, taking a fork that eliminated the steep uphill to Little Copper Butte, and dropped down to a paradise within a paradise...a huge wildflower-filled cirque, complete with a spring gushing out of the mountainside. A super hidden-away spot, we knew we'd be back some day. The path out of the private cove led us back to Trail #602, our ticket back to our mountaintop home. Trying to make it back before dark, we only stopped once in the next six miles, at a spring we found on the west side of Copper Butte. Then it was into Mica Saddle and a long trudge up to the Indian Hill Trailhead, making it back to our wilderness home and Fritz, as the sun sank beneath the horizon out over Oregon.

July 15th

My favorite spot to go before I checked in with Fenn Dispatch at 0800, was to the top of the bluffs three hundred yards from the lookout. It was close by, and had a terrific view of not only the wilderness, but of the firetower. Sometimes I'd go with Judy and sometimes by myself. Today I was going with our little buddy. A hundred feet uphill of the bluffs was a large camping flat that appeared to be a favorite spot for the hunters—meat poles were strung up in the trees, a few campfire rings, and leftover hay was strewn about on the ground. Fritz followed along, as we made our way through the hunters' camps and down to the top of the bluffs.

At the top of the fifty-foot drop-off I sat down on a rocky ledge, holding onto our cat, gazing out over a million acres of wilderness at my feet. I looked out to Otter Butte across the Otter Creek valley, Highline Ridge at the head of the valley, then the Crags that always left me speechless. Bearwallow Lookout, a twin of Indian Hill on a 41-foot tower, and Shissler Peak Lookout, a twin of Coolwater with a 10-foot tower, sat on prominent points out across the snaking Selway River. Then I took in the special view of our home sweet home for the summer. We were so lucky to be living on a mountaintop. And I couldn't thank Judy enough for going along with me to try out this totally unique lifestyle. I thought about it...our 1st wedding anniversary, August 11th, was less than a month away. I'd have to do something special on that special day. And I knew exactly what that was. Not wanting to test my luck with letting go of Fritz, I carried my little buddy until the hunter flats, then he followed me back home.

    The July 9th storm wasn't through with us just yet, as a couple holdover fires popped up for me to report to Fenn. It became my entertainment—when Fritz wasn't outside—to feed the Columbian and cute little Golden Mantled ground squirrels leftover pancakes. I had all the Golden Mantles named...Rocky 1, Rocky 2, and Rocky 3. Every day it was a constant lookout for fires, scanning my country every twenty minutes. More lightning storms came sweeping in from Oregon, though none that could hold a candle to the BIG ONE on the 9th! Visitors kept trickling up to the lookout, mostly on weekends. I would point out the country and describe to them the "life of a lookout". Most everybody only stayed for about fifteen minutes, until Tim and Sally showed up. They announced that they were going to be staying for nearly a whole week! They must have seen our jaws drop when they told us that. But it wasn't as bad as we feared...they camped on the hunter flat, and spent their days exploring the mountaintop, much like us. Our "hippie neighbors" even invited us down to sit around the campfires, and we reciprocated, inviting them up to enjoy the view from the lookout. But even though it wasn't as bad as we feared, we were oh so glad to see them leave and have the mountaintop to ourselves once again.

🐝 July 23rd 1400 hours

Our peace was suddenly broken by the sound of a rig grinding its way up the mountain. Louder and louder it got until we could finally see it rounding the corner by the start of the spring trail, and going down the last stretch of our 12-mile-long driveway. Something looked quite familiar with that rig. Of course! It was a Forest Service green pickup! They drove up and parked in front of the log cabin. Nerves surfaced as I saw Wick step out of the pickup. Then I saw Bonnie and Al Schonefeld, a couple of trail surveyors, get out, taking out a couple of backpacks from the bed of the truck and putting them on the porch. Wick, with clipboard in hand, got some cans of paint out of the back of the truck, and placed them by the packs. Then the three of them started up the lookout path, heading our way.

"Hey Crawford!" Wick yelled up to me as I stared down at them. "Got the coffee on?"

Coffee...coffee. Darn! It was the one thing we didn't bring as neither of us drank coffee. "Sorry, but there's no coffee up here!"

Soon three sets of footsteps vibrated the firetower, as they made their way up to the top.

"Need to replace some of those steps!" Wick said as he broke through the catwalk opening.

Trying to not show my nervousness from what was obviously an inspection, I gave a firm handshake to my boss. "Hi guys," I greeted the trail workers whom I had met before we came up to the lookout.

"Hi!" Judy also greeted our guests.

"I see you guys have been busy peeling paint this summer!" Wick noted.

"We do a little bit every day!" I proudly admitted.

"Good. Well, I put some paint on the cabin porch for you, Crawford. Can't let the wood show over winter."

"We'll get it painted," I replied.

The inspection started with Wick going over my fire detection reports, lightning strike records, and false and legitimate smoke forms. Then he reviewed my official daily logbook, making a comment to be a little neater. Then he asked me how to locate a fire at night using the panoramic photos I had in the firefinder cabinet. I went over the details of night fire detection…how to use the 360-degree azimuth firefinder ring and the 20-degree vertical angle scale to plot it on the photo. He checked to see if I had my orientation points posted on the firefinder cabinet…check.

Then suddenly a thought popped into my mind! I *hadn't* done a lookout since they got here. So I excused myself, and went out on the catwalk, checking out my country on all four sides. All was quiet…no smokes showing in my seen area. So far so good. I was hoping beyond hope that those two flubs during the first week up here—the 4-5 screw-up and the missed practice fire—wouldn't be held against me. When I went back inside Wick complimented me on how well I did on that big lightning bust. And he had me beaming with the firefighting report from Smith and Hayes. He handed me a copy of the inspection form that I passed, which made my day! Wick left with another reminder to keep a close eye on the area below me down in Meadow Creek.

"You sure looked nervous!" Al commented as Wick made his way down the four flights of stairs.

"I *was* nervous as heck," I proclaimed. "Sure glad that's over!"

"You guys mind if we stay in the cabin tonight?" Bonnie

asked.

"Yeah, we're heading out on another 10-day hitch first thing in the morning," Al added.

"Sure, the cabin's all yours, if you don't mind a few mice running around tonight."

"A few mice won't bother us!" Bonnie announced. "Just so long as there aren't any pack rats down there!"

"Thank goodness I haven't seen any rats yet."

It felt like a thousand-pound weight was lifted off my shoulders with Wick not holding the two earlier screw-ups against me. Bonnie and Al and Judy and I had an enjoyable evening visiting with them talking about their trail survey work, and Judy and I talking about our lookout adventures. At 0600 the next morning, they were off down the road with some heavy packs, heading on their 10-day hitch.

By the end of July our refrigerator and cupboards were looking a little bare. Long gone was all the fresh meat we had brought up with us. Gone were all the fruit and vegetables. Nearly gone were all the canned goods, and even the dry goods like rice, noodles, powdered milk, and flour were running low. And we had to shop for my Mom and Dad's visit. In the mail that Wick brought up, was a letter from my parents announcing that they'd be coming up here on or around our anniversary. So Judy went off on an eight-hour round trip to the tiny town of Kooskia on a resupply run.

🐝 *August 11th*

I got up with the sun peeking up over the Bitterroots, carefully making my way over my still zonked-out wife, on a mission to go to the alpine florist. As quiet as a church mouse, I put Fritz's collar on with his bell, and he followed me out the door, down the four flights and the lookout path to the cabin. Grabbing a kitchen knife that I found, we continued on our way to the twenty-acre meadow. We got to the start of the spring trail and headed south until we hit a fork. Fritz kept going straight, as if we were going for water. I grabbed my little buddy and put him on the meadow path that he had been on only a couple of times. Letting him go again, we continued along the trail, going through beargrass, and around lodgepoles and alpine firs to get to the beautiful flower-filled hillside. Soon we were at the meadow where Judy and I had gone many times this summer after hours. Red, purple, yellow, orange, and white flowers danced in the slight breeze that started up. Fritz checked on some ground squirrel holes, while I went to work cutting a bouquet of penstemon, larkspur, Indian Paintbrush, sulphurflower, pearly everlasting, and some flowers that I couldn't identify. Once I got two handfuls I tore Fritz away from some ground squirrel diggings and pointed him back uphill.

Back at the log cabin I completed my mission by making an anniversary card out of the paper that I had brought down yesterday. I folded the typewriter paper in half. On the front I drew a picture of a series of hills with a lookout tower on the last one. Then inside I wrote…

Thanks Hon for coming on this adventure with me. Happy 1st Anniversary!

Love John

I put the flowers in an old coffee pot I got from the top of the cookstove and made my way up the lookout path to our summer home, with Fritz clinging and clanging, running ahead. Out of breath at the top of the tower climb, I noticed Judy was already up and going.

"Happy Anniversary, Hon!" I said, handing her the coffee pot of flowers.

"Oh...thank you John!" she exclaimed. "I wondered where you went so early this morning." She set the flowers down and gave me a big hug.

Then I handed her the card.

After she read it she handed me the card she'd made for me. Drawn on the front were some wildflowers and inside she wrote...

Happy 1st Anniversary, John!

Love, Judy

I hugged her back and gave her a kiss.

Amidst the grandeur of the wilderness, sitting on top of the world at Indian Hill, we had a nice hot shower, with each of us holding the beach towel to shield us from the light easterly breeze.

We ended up having a special anniversary supper, with a couple steaks that Judy bought on her resupply run. Then we got a surprise visit from Rhondy and Sandy Lyons, who we made friends with before the lookout season down at Fenn, bringing us a bottle of wine. Spending the rest of the evening visiting with friends and sipping on a Cabernet, it was a great ending to a very special day.

🌲 August 13th

It wasn't like I didn't want to see my parents and brother. It was just that I was their taxi driver up to the lookout and I didn't want to be going up the steep road in this driving rain. It was getting slick already as I made my way down to meet them at Slim's Camp, and it was only going to be getting slicker!

I recognized their car as I made my way down the steepest section of road at the bottom. Then I saw three hands waving.

"Great to see you guys!" I said, opening the station wagon door and giving Dad and Mom a big hug.

"Great to see you too, son!" Dad and Mom chorused.

"How's it going, Jeff?" I asked.

"Not bad."

With all three of us dressed for the weather with rain coats on, we traded some notes about their trip, and their plans to check out the World's Fair in Spokane when they left the lookout. Then came the moment of truth, as they transferred their suitcases and sleeping bags and pillows into the station wagon, and we started up our long driveway.

The first mile up the steep mountain road went smoothly, with enough rock in the roadway to give us traction. Then came a steep, muddy and rutted-out section where I needed speed to make it through. What I really needed was a set of chains, which I didn't have. Or my head examined for not waiting a few hours to let the rain soak into the roadbed. I gunned it just enough to get momentum through the first mudhole. Getting a little bit of speed on the rare flat section on the first switchback, I said a little prayer that we'd make it. Hitting the steep, muddy ruts, my nearly bald highway tires were spinning, losing much-needed traction. Stuck in the ruts, I just barely made it to another fairly flat section. One look over at Mom and Dad told the whole story...they were scared stiff! Losing traction and not getting up the mountain was one thing, but slipping off the edge and falling down into the deep Selway canyon was quite another thing! I tightened my vice-grip on the steering wheel, making sure to keep it on the road. I remembered one more sketchy mudhole and switchback from the trip down, halfway up the mountain.

I hit the long, deeply rutted mudhole with enough speed to get me past it and make the tight right-turn switchback. I kept the pedal to the metal, spinning and slipping and sliding my way through the mud bog. Then the switchback. With just enough momentum I coaxed the Pontiac beyond the tight turn and thankfully to the more mellow upper half of the road as I continued up our driveway. I pointed out where I fought the fire, then we stopped at the Little Creek mini falls for a picture and a drink. Then I showed them the horse trough spring where we got our water, the Meadow Creek and Copper Butte Trailheads, and finally the lookout tower playing peek-a-boo in the fog.

Judy met us at the log cabin, giving her in-laws a great big hug. Then we helped them settle into their temporary living quarters, with Jeff taking the loft cot, and Mom and Dad laying out their sleeping bags below on the mattress-covered steel bunks. I was secretly holding out hope that the mouse house "residents" wouldn't scamper all over my sleeping parents.

It was like old home week on the mountaintop, catching my parents up on what's been happening at the lookout, and hearing about their trip out west. Then we took them to our favorite places...going to the meadow, then to the top of the bluffs, and checking out the patrol point, where Jeff made a cairn to add to the one already there. With Judy and Mom staying at the lookout, Dad, Jeff and I took a hike out past Copper Butte, meeting up with a trail crew that was working on making new tread. Then, on the last day of their visit, Dad and Jeff took up my suggestion to hike down Trail #603 to Meadow Creek and out to Slim's Camp where we would meet them for a picnic supper. I insisted that it would be all downhill, so it *shouldn't* be too hard. The minute I watched them disappear from sight heading down the trail at the switchback a mile from the tower, I was thinking that maybe they bit off a little more than they could chew. Yes, it was all downhill, according to the topo's, but it was a good fifteen mile hike, and Dad was in his 50's. The rest of the afternoon at the lookout I felt a little twinge of guilt of sending them on something I hadn't even hiked.

Our rendezvous time was 1800, so we packed up all their gear from the cabin, and within the hour were down at Slim's Camp and the end of the trail, hoping like heck we'd see them waiting for us. But no such luck.

"They did say they'd meet us at six," Mom asked, looking about as anxious as I was.

"Yeah...that was the time they were expected to be out."

"I'm sure they'll show up anytime now!" Judy added, trying to sound upbeat.

While waiting for them to appear, we transferred all their stuff into the trunk of their car, then laid out the plastic tablecloth on a picnic table, putting rocks on the corners so that it wouldn't blow away. I put a couple of canteens with fresh spring water on the table.

A half an hour went by before I made a decision to start hiking up the trail to see where the heck they were. Hiking faster than normal, I virtually jogged up the trail to find the wilderness wanderers. About a half mile from the trailhead I finally caught sight of my brother.

"Hey Jeff! Am I glad to see you! Where's Dad?" I gasped, out of breath.

"He's a ways back there yet. That was a pretty tough hike for him!" Jeff said convincingly.

"Jeff...you're only about a half mile from Slim's Camp. Why don't you go on and let Mom and Judy know that I'll try to find Dad."

Running now to find my father who I felt could be in serious trouble, I rounded bend after bend in the trail, paralleling the beautiful, rushing Meadow Creek. When I thought my heart was going to beat out of my chest, I took a breather. "Hey Dad!" I yelled as best as I could up the trail where I was hoping beyond hope that Dad would appear at any moment. "Dad!" I yelled again with as much breath as I could muster.

"Johnnnn..." I could faintly hear.

"Dad!" Not waiting for a response, I ran like a deer up the rocky trail, hoping that my father was okay.

"John!" I heard it loud and clear this time.

Tripping over more rocks and roots, I kept up my frantic pace until thankfully I met up with my Dad who was leaning over with both hands on his knees, totally spent.

"Thanks for checking on me, son!" Dad said sounding about as winded as me.

"Oh, you bet, Dad! I was worried sick about you and so was Mom."

"That trail was beautiful! All those huge pines coming down off Indian Hill and these gigantic, beautiful cedars down along Meadow Creek!"

"Yeah, these cedars sure are impressive."

"I probably bit off a little more than I could chew. Glad I'm almost at the end of the trail!" Dad said, still out of breath.

"I probably shouldn't have pushed you guys into going that far, Dad."

"I *am* glad that we went. It was sure some beautiful country!"

"You've got only about a mile to go."

"Is Jeff up ahead?"

"Yeah...he went to tell Mom and Judy that I was looking for you."

Slow but sure we finally made it out to the trailhead. Amongst the huge cedars that Dad so loved, we had our picnic, cooking hot dogs on sticks over a fire. We said goodbye to my parents and Jeff, who were on their way to Spokane and the World's Fair. Judy and I waved as they drove over the Meadow Creek bridge and disappeared from sight.

Life on the mountaintop kept rolling along, with a couple more storms rocking the lookout ridge in the last half of August, one happening in the middle of the night. Proving that lightning can hit twice in the same spot, we got yet another direct strike on the tower, momentarily blinding us, sounding like someone shot a rifle right next to our ears. When our vision returned we could see St. Elmo's Fire, with the shutter bolts and antennae glowing in the dark. Projects got done, replacing some of the cracked steps with 2x10's I found in the attic of the cabin, and the railing and lookout got a fresh coat of white paint. We went out huckleberry picking along Trail #603, where the bushes were loaded down with them. Then we started getting regular visits by the local outfitter, Jack Dark, who set up camp down by the Meadow Creek Trailhead. Clearing the Otter Butte Trail to his hunting spike camps, we got to hear about what it was like down in Otter Creek, and about some bighorn sheep he spotted across the valley. We continued to see elk and deer, and the occasional moose making their way through the five-acre clearing around the tower. On about September 10th a trickle of hunters started ascending the mountain to get ready for the hunting season. Then the trickle became a flood, as our peace and solitude was no more. They came in pickups, pickup campers, pickups hauling horse trailers, and in stock trucks, loaded down with horses and mules. Tens of hunters came, camping in every conceivable spot...at the trailhead, wedging in down at the saddle where the patrol point trail took off, squeezing into the camp flat above the bluffs. And even onto the small camp flat just past the corral, which was way too close for comfort! The lookout ridge became a hub of activity...hunters sighting in their rifles, horses whinnying and mules heehawing, chopping wood, nailing up yet more meat poles, digging latrine pits, setting up wall tents. And they came, one after another, climbing the tower steps to ask me a bunch of questions..."Where's the elk?" "Seen any big bears around here?" "Any mulie bucks around?" It all led up to September 15th, the opening day of hunting season, when more shots rang out over the land, and some of the elk and deer we'd been seeing all summer got harvested.

🐝 September 18th 1430 hours

It was the strangest sight I'd seen in my short fire lookout career, when I was doing a lookout to the east of the tower and saw what I *couldn't* believe—three smokes, all in a row, appearing just below Highline Ridge! "Hey Jude...look out here!"

My wife hurried out on the catwalk from making some bread. "Holy cow!" she exclaimed. "What the heck is that all about?"

"Not sure, but they definitely aren't holdover fires!"

"Better get a legal and call them in!"

"Right away!"

Appearing around the bend in the road by the hunter camp flat, I saw a guy on a horse galloping towards us, racing for the lookout. Like some kind of Western flick, he brought the horse to an abrupt halt at the start of the lookout path and jumped off, yelling up to me..."My buddy's been shot out by Highline! You need to call for a chopper right away!"

"I'm on it!" I yelled back down to the guy who was running up the path.

I bolted inside and grabbed the hand-held mike and urgently radioed Dispatch. "Fenn, this is Indian Hill!" I nervously spoke.

"Indian Hill, this is Fenn." The winded cowboy appeared in the doorway.

"Yeah, I've got a guy up here who says his buddy was shot out by Highline…"

"Through the femoral artery!" he exclaimed, gasping for breath.

"He was shot through the femoral artery just below Highline Ridge! They need a helicopter as soon as possible! There's three smokes out there now showing where to land."

"The helicopter will be dispatched right away!" they responded.

"10-4, Fenn."

"ETA in about a half an hour. KOC-271."

"Indian Hill clear."

Anxiously we waited until we saw the tiny helicopter make its way up Otter Creek and land up on Highline Ridge, just above the three signal fires. Then when the copter left, the friend of the guy who got shot, jumped back on his horse and made his way back down the road.

By the end of September most of the hunters had left, finally giving us our peace and quiet back. No longer would we have to fear for our lives just going to the outhouse and on our walks. Vibrant reds, purples, and brilliant yellows and oranges adorned the mountainsides, the fall colors showing across the countryside. We quit taking showers on the catwalk with the colder weather, changing instead to doing sponge baths in the lookout, with the oven door open. We ended our days, glued to the radio, listening to the evening Breeze Session to hear what our lookout neighbors were up to, their voices warming the airwaves.

🌲 October 18th 2100 hours

An early-winter storm dumped eight inches of snow on the mountaintop, our world in a thick gray blanket of fog, squelching out the fire season for good. Down in the log cabin, Doug Green and Bob Moore, the Copper Butte trail crew, were taking refuge, sitting around the woodstove to keep warm. Fritz was keeping warm in his kapok sleeping-bag tent while Judy and I were snug as a bug in a rug in our eight-blanketed lookout bed.

"Where do you think we should live this winter?" I asked my bride, pulling up the covers to my chin to ward off the chill in the lookout.

"I haven't got a clue! Let's just flip a coin and decide whether to go to Lewiston or Missoula when we get down to Fenn."

"Sounds good to me."

The soft sound of snow hitting the west windows lulled me off to sleep.

🐝 *October 19th 0700 hours*

    I snuck out from my warm cocoon and peeked out at the mountaintop. Fog still hugged the ridge, but thankfully the snow had stopped. I could see smoke rising out of the cabin's chimney. Our neighbors were awake.

    Soon Judy hopped out of bed onto the ice-cold linoleum floor, starting the oven to get some heat in the frigid lookout house. We both put on the cold clothes we had piled at the foot of the bed, and then fed our meowing cat. Expecting the crew who soon would be coming up to help close the lookout down for the winter, there was no time to waste. After a quick oatmeal breakfast we began the process of getting all the stuff we'd brought up in June ready to be hauled down. Bedding got folded and put on the bed. Clothes got boxed up. As did all the books we had read this summer. Leftover canned goods and dry goods boxed up. The firefinder oiled for the long winter ahead. The freezer defrosted and refrigerator cleaned. The stove, and then the oven cleaned. Like clockwork Jerry Rieman and Johnny Smith of the fire crew arrived at 0900 to take us down.

    It was a whirlwind of activity now, carefully hauling all the boxes down the slippery lookout steps, cautiously letting down the heavy, snow-laden shutters and nailing them down, and then officially going 10-7 for the season over the Forest net, by far the saddest moment of the lookout season. Everything done, we locked the door and headed out...Johnny and Jerry first, with Judy and myself following right behind. After we locked the catwalk gate and climbed down to the third landing, Fritz had other ideas, and climbed back up to the gate, meowing to get back in his home.

    "No, little buddy...we're heading to a different home now. I climbed back and picked him up and carried him down, sadly leaving our summer home for the next eight months. I took down the flag and rain bucket and the lookout sign and put them in the log cabin. After a snowball fight with Bob and Doug, and the log cabin shutters secured, and a can put on the stove pipe, we locked the door and were ready to head down the mountain. Taking one last glance back at the lookout, it looked so lonely all boarded up, without its residents. Then I *saw* something else...I *saw* the helicopter landing again in the soft bed of phlox that adorned the ridge, and Judy, Fritz and I being let off to live like the Swiss Family Robinson once again. As I left the mountaintop that day, I knew it *wasn't* over after all. It was merely the beginning!

   My vision proved true, as I continued to return to Indian Hill for the next 35 years.

   On Indian Hill, in the summer of 1975, I had a couple guys drive up in a pickup and get out. The guy who was sitting in the passenger seat appeared excited to see me. He immediately shook my hand firmly and announced..."*Thank you so much for saving my life!*"

   At first I didn't put two and two together, but then he went on to explain that he was the guy who got shot last fall in the wilderness. I was swelling with pride knowing that by calling for that helicopter rescue that I had indeed saved the man's life.

Helicopter landing at Indian Hill

Fritz welcoming visitors to the lookout

The phlox ground cover

Blooming beargrass

Ground strikes to the west

Judy on clothes washing day

Looking for forest fires

Jeff and Dad at the trailhead heading out on Meadow Creek hike in 1974

Elk grazing below the lookout

Plotting fires on ceiling map

Snow sliding on Little Copper Butte ridge with the Crags in the distance

1998

🌲 July 5ᵗʰ Day 1

1030 hours   A welcoming mat of pink, purple and white phlox groundcover greets my arrival to Indian Hill. I breathe in deeply, absorbing the heavenly alpine aroma, and take in the breathtaking Montana-to-Oregon view. The Forest Service crew that arrived earlier helps me move into my 41-foot-tall, all-glass-walled lookout in the sky.

1310 hours   The crew leaves me alone on my mountaintop perch as I feel a severing of my ties to civilization. Listening closely, I can hear the sounds of the mountaintop come alive…the snowmelt cascading over slabs of rock in the steep-walled basin to my east, the cry of a red-tailed hawk soaring high above the lookout ridge, the beautiful song serenade of a bird soloist I've named the lark of the mountain.

🌲 July 8ᵗʰ Day 4

1610 hours   Sitting on my glass-insulated lightning stool, I can feel the firetower's wooden legs moving under me with each new pulse from the storm that's buffeting the ridge. Lightning strikes stab at the thickly forested mountainsides around my summer home, igniting flare-ups, sending short-lived columns of gray-black smoke into the prematurely darkened sky. Curved veils of moisture sweep out of the massive cloud, dousing any chance of a serious forest fire starting in the area.

   Suddenly a bright flash of light blinds me, instantly followed by a deafening BANG that rattles the thin-paned windows. The feel of electricity fills my 14x14-foot home, a tingling sensation happening in the back of my neck. The storm intensifies, jagged-lined multiple lightning strikes jabbing at the deep fissures in the earth. More fires start, then quickly get snuffed out by the rain. Next to the tower the tops of the alpine firs get swept over, looking like they soon will be part of the forest floor. Then they straighten themselves like a sailboat keeling back to an upright position.

1745 hours   The storm finally moves north, out of my area. Puffs of moisture begin to form in the branching tributaries of the Selway River, some looking suspiciously like smoke. I study each wisp of moisture until I'm satisfied nothing is burning.

1945 hours   I radio Coolwater Lookout to compare notes about what appears to be a smoke in the head of Island Creek. The lookout confirms what I suspected, then radios the fire detection report down to Fenn Ranger Station.

2054 hours   A red-ball sunset melts into the horizon, accentuating the dark gray curtains of rain from storms far off to my west.

July 12th Day 8

As if on command, the storms of the past week come to an abrupt halt. In their wake, a dozen small forest fires have been started, and hundreds of blown-over trees are blocking area trails. A shutter from Shissler Peak Lookout was last seen flying like a giant leaf into the valley to his east.

My life on the mountaintop is settling into a sort of routine. Mountain spring visits happen at least once a week for a fresh supply of 25 gallons of water. Sponge baths are taken twice a week. Once-used bath water is used to wash the floor. The Osborne Firefinder is oriented weekly to ensure accurate fire locations.

🐝 July 24th Day 20

0415 hours The tower gets hit with what the clouds and wind had forecast...rain, wind and cloud-to-cloud lightning waking me before dawn.

🐝 August 4th Day 31

My parents, sister Carol and her husband, Rich, my nephew Michael and my niece Becca, show up for a much looked-forward-to visit. Coolwater Lookout keeps an extra watchful eye on my area as I get the day off the tower to meet my family on the Selway River, a 15-mile drive down a steep, narrow road. Inflating five truck inner tubes and a small raft, we make a small flotilla, lazily floating down the emerald green river, stopping at a pristine white-sand beach to have a picnic lunch.

🐝 August 7th Day 34

On their second and last trip up the mountain from a bed and breakfast, a two-hour drive from the tower, my parents' visit coincides with seeing the after-effects of the largest storm of the summer.

Mom and Dad are recruited to help detect forest fires. By the end of the day we have spotted eight more holdover lightning fires, plotting their locations on the Osborne Firefinder. Ranger Station fire crews and smokejumpers are dispatched to put out the fires reported by me and other nearby lookouts.

🐝 August 13th Day 40

The day begins with a warm pinkish glow angling through the jagged crest of the Bitterroot Mountains, 60 air-miles away.

All is quiet, the bird soloists of July already leaving for parts unknown. Only the slightest whisper of water can be heard cascading down into the Bluff Creek Valley on the Selway Bitterroot Wilderness side of my tower.

Soon I can hear my home being used as an aerial playground for nuthatches, the *na na na* of the little aviators coming from the guy-wire perches on the tower beneath me. A fluffed-out little bird lands on the railing, three feet from my head, looking through the glass at me. We both stare at each other until he flutters off to the cross braces below. The *na na na's* last for another ten minutes, then the mountaintop becomes quiet again.

1400 hours   Sitting on the west side catwalk, I can feel the wind picking up from out of the northwest. A red-tail hawk uses the invisible air currents like a giant waterslide, climbing steeply into the stiff breeze, then coming to an abrupt stop in mid-air, pulling its wings back and diving for the evergreen spires along the ridge. At the bottom of the slide, he puts his wings out and arcs back to the heavens to do another roller-coaster ride in the wind current.

My routine of scanning my area for fires is only broken up now with short stints of window washing, scraping paint on the lookout building and reading one of the many books I brought up for the summer. Every twenty minutes I look out and search the mountains for the small residue of blue smoke that would trigger me into action.

Patiently I wait.

🐾 *August 15th Day 42*

2100 hours   A bear can be heard beneath the firetower, his claws tearing apart a half-rotten log on the ground. I double check to make sure the trapdoor was secured for the night.

🐾 *August 19th Day 46*

1530 hours   Suspicious-looking blue haze is spotted in the canyon, about a mile to my northeast. I suspect it's smoke from a forest fire, but am unable to find its source.

1730 hours   My fire watch vigil into Bluff Creek pays off as I spot a moderate-sized column of blue-gray smoke rise up from below the tower. Immediately I line up the fire on the firefinder, getting a bearing and location before reporting it to the ranger station.

1800 hours   I get a bird's eye view of four smokejumpers floating to the ground, landing in a clearing above the fire. Three jumpers hit the opening. But one misses and gets hung up in a tree, dangling from the parachute that looks like a huge blue-and-white flag flapping in the wind. For two days, the firefighters fight the blaze under my lookout, digging fire lines, beating back flames and churning up hot soil. On August 21st, the fire is officially declared out and one lone fire lookout above them breathes one big sigh of relief.

🐾 *August 25th Day 52*

1330 hours   Two bighorn sheep can be seen feeding off to the northwest of the firetower. Between lookouts for smokes, I keep close tabs on my new neighbors.

🌲 September 7th Day 65

Lightning storms start a new series of forest fires in the dry evergreen forest to my west. Just as one of the fires starts taking off, a general rain hits the area and quiets what could have been a major blaze.

🌲 September 19th Day 77

1600 hours Snow sweeps by my windows, starting to stick on the railings and catwalk. The fire that is crackling next to me in the woodstove can barely offset the cold outside my walls of glass.

🌲 September 20th Day 78

0700 hours I look out over the Selway River Valley, which is a sea of fog, and see the mountaintop islands, including my own, covered with a fresh dusting of snow. The wind is still. Nothing can be heard. The dead silence of late fall/early winter has arrived to the high country.

I know that soon I'll be heading down off the mountaintop, returning to the western Montana valley where I built a log-sided house. There I'll spend my winter working on the house in the country and writing of my outdoor adventures.

But come next spring, I'll look up from the valley floor to the mountains and get excited again. Because I know that I will once again be returning to my paradise up on Indian Hill.

Till next summer…

 2001

September 9th Day 71

1600 hours   The northwest breeze eddies around my lookout, feeling its way through the west-side shutters.

Over two months into my twenty-eighth summer on Indian Hill, I'm psychologically preparing myself for another nine-month-long stay in civilization. But it's tough. Indian summer is at its best. Warm days. Cool nights. No bugs. And no people bugging me. The Selway Crags are painted with the rusts of the sorrel, the bright reds of the huckleberry, the yellows of the cured-out grasses, the deepening shadows behind the steep rocky ridges of the high lake basins. A Cessna's drone peaks, then starts to fade as it makes its way down the Selway Valley, returning to Kamiah, Orofino or Lewiston from the Moose Creek backcountry airstrip. The wind increases; the whispering turning into a whistling sound.

2030 hours   The Coleman lantern hisses away, the standard-issue Forest Service light offering just enough illumination to read. I keep my head into the book until the government radio interrupts as it has done several times already tonight. Some law enforcement officer is talking to dispatch, trying to figure out the whereabouts of the security people being sent down to him. Twenty-eight years of being the Indian Hill Lookout, I've heard and seen a lot. But never this. An arsonist. A very "good" arsonist. For three days now, he has kept the security folks guessing, trying to figure out the mind of this pyromaniac. Where's he going to strike next? When? Day one saw five fires start. Day two three fires. Day three, one fire. From my perch on the mountaintop I'm trying to be the detective of this bizarre case. Nine fires in three days! Shortly after Pilot Knob Lookout, the closest fire watch into the South Fork of the Clearwater River, announced he was going out of service, the fire in the South Fork started.

Coincidence? Or is this guy monitoring the Forest Service radio network? The Sherlock Holmes of Indian Hill. Maybe it was all those Hardy Boy books that I read as a kid.

Another five security folks are being mobilized in Grangeville. I think I'll let them handle things and go back to reading. Back to Pete Fromm's *King On The Mountain*. Not one of his better works in my opinion. But I'm not sure if my best writing is as good as his worst writing.

Thoughts drift away from Fromm's creative wanderings and center on Judy. My best friend. My confidante. My everything. Even though we weren't married anymore, I miss her dearly.

I carry the thoughts of Judy and our cat family with me. The many years of Judy and I, and Fritz, Rhoda and Fluffy together. We helicoptered up with Fritz on our first year on lookout, in 1974. Rhoda joined the Crawford clan in 1979, a little orange long-haired ball of fluff that fell in love with Judy and Judy with her. Fluffy was the third cat "kid" we adopted.

The lantern chugs away. I pick up Fromm again and try to erase the feelings that are welling up from my aching heart. But reading is not erasing any of the sadness. It's time to go to bed and dream of the day Judy returns to our nest high above the Selway River.

🐾 *September 10th Day 72*

0830 hours   I'm at work, sitting on my deck chair, looking at the view. My job...scanning the scene before me, the Bitterroot Mountain Range of Montana on my eastern horizon, the Wallowa Mountain Range of Oregon, over a hundred air miles away, on my western horizon and the millions of acres of the earth inbetween folded every which way that forms the mural before my eyes. Swallows are dive-bombing the tower, using my house as a target in their game of who can come the closest. I reach out and almost touch one of the daredevil pilots, the little aviator doing an abrupt ninety-degree turn away from me at the last possible moment. Then another swallow slips in the heels of the last attack, pulling left just before he splats into my railing. The day is calm. Not even a wind whisper.

    I yawn...tired from a night of the tower swaying back and forth on its forty-one-foot legs. Fall breeds wind that brings the hawks to soar on the thermals, clears the air of any smoke, makes me feel so alive. But last night's strong winds kept me thinking what it would be like to land in a big heap on the ground, the glass shrapnel slicing what's left of my smashed body to shreds. No, not much sleep.

    I finish my first official scan of the day. The arsonist must be sleeping. Or reading the Lewiston Morning Tribune about his fire-starting spree (I never found out if they caught the guy). There aren't any new fires that I can detect. And the other lookouts are quiet. Everything is as it should be, Smokey the Bear doing his job. Nothing's burning except for what they're calling the Earthquake Fire. That's burning quite well this morning. Retardant ships and helicopters are diving in and out of the fire that still sounds like it isn't controlled.

    Na na na na na. A nuthatch is dangling from the tower. I feel like I'm in a tree, they hardly pay any attention to me. He flies off. His buddies join him.

🐝 September 12th Day 74

    1400 hours   I can only make out the sound of a fly buzzing as he erratically makes a tour of the catwalk. Another fly buzz. Then they leave to check out some other spot. Not a sound now. The wind isn't even fluttering the flag.

Complete silence. The silence that makes me feel as isolated as I am, miles from nowhere. Cumulus clouds build in the southwestern sky, white cauliflower-edged clouds against a backdrop of azure blue. A perfect lookout day normally. But this is anything but a normal day. It's a day of mourning. Sadness wraps this nation like a huge fifty-state quilt...every American in a state of shock over what happened yesterday. With no AM/FM radio and a rare day off, I was clueless until a hunter informed me of the tragedy in New York and Washington. Terrorists commandeering four civilian airplanes, suicide-bombing two of them into the World Trade Center one into the Pentagon, and one into a Pennsylvania field. I couldn't believe my ears. About as removed from yesterday's tragic events as anyone could be, but as affected as any American, I spend the day thinking about what I'd heard and praying for the people's families of those who lost their lives.

The flag I fly proudly, half mast out of respect for the slain people, begins to flutter with the northwest breeze, like God is responding to my feelings of loss for the United States as a country.

My gray jay buddies add a little joy to an otherwise sad day. They're perched in the tops of the nearby fir trees, calling to me to get fed. Out of bread and out of crackers, I toss out a broken-off section of a pancake I saved from breakfast. Bird number one does a swan dive out of the alpine fir tree top and gracefully arcs down to intersect with the morsel of food that's already hit the ground. Birds two and three squawk a complaint and another piece of huckleberry pancake goes flying. The two birds leap at the same time off their perches and compete for the one piece that lands on the boardwalk below. The jay that's lost out flies up to a new perch, settling on the northeast guide wire, getting closer to the guy in the sky who's got the goodies. I fling out one last piece and he swoops down to almost catch it before it hits the ground. Hopping on the rock-landing spot, he quickly pecks at it, securing it in his mouth. Then off he flies, following his buddies to the nearby forest to find a suitable tree to cache his pancake with the other crackers, cookies, bread sections and pancake pieces. They quickly return for another round of handouts and I oblige them until the pancake is gone on the third round of feeding.

The cumulus clouds are continuing to build. If I didn't know better, it has a feel of July to it. 73 degrees. The middle-of-summer type of warmth. How I wish. It seems like the summer never really got going. No fire-starting thunderstorms on the Moose Creek District I work for. It was a "slow" year. The slowest in twenty-eight summers. One fire to my credit and that went out. I'm beginning to feel like the May Tag repairman up here. So these darkening clouds are my last rays of hope, my last gasp at finding a lightning-caused fire. And my last chance at strengthening the justification for having me up here. Over the years I've averaged around fifteen fires per season on Indian Hill. I just hope that they remember those years and not this one. Otherwise my job could be in jeopardy.

Nostalgia is everywhere I look. In front of me is the old table stand I cut out of a log for having breakfasts on the deck with Judy. Scratched into the base are the cat family's claw marks. The stove hearth I built, with the names John, Judy, Fritz, Rhoda, and Fluffy etched into the mortar. The names I've got etched into everything else—and the dates—on the entrance sign, the logs in the log cabin, the old metal mileage marker on the trail north of the tower, the attic boards. And places I've forgotten about. Our names are a constant reminder of the many years we've spent together on Indian Hill.

Darn! I'm getting lonely again. Better divert my thoughts.

🌲 September 13th Day 75

1230 hours   My last fire hope is building on my southwestern horizon in the form of puffy white cumulus clouds. They're lined out perfect for a mid-afternoon storm coming across our District. If this were July, I'd bank on it happening. A September lightning storm is rare, and even more rare is to get a fire starting from any of them. I sit here and wish for one final exclamation point to an otherwise uneventful fire season. Like waiting for water to boil, I can't keep staring at these clouds or they'll go away, dissipating into yet another non-storm event.

The wind is barely visible, the flag barely wiggling from its nearly limp status. I can't hear Meadow Creek, a vertical mile to my west. If the wind picks up, I know it will usher the water sounds to my perch.

Clouds are continuing to build. "Keep your head down, Crawford!" I yell to the bird-and-chipmunk audience that's eating seeds from the local foliage. "Don't look!" But I take another peek at the clouds after another reminder not to.

Bread is fresh out of the oven. The second of my baking efforts for the lookout season looks good, but the bulletproof crust could probably be used for the outer layer of a bomb shelter. I might need a hacksaw for the latest homemade bread effort.

The clouds are making animal shapes, one looking like a giant poodle, another a turkey roasting in the oven, complete with puffy-white drumsticks. Still no lightning. Still building hopes, not fires.

The Columbian ground squirrels are in bed now, the earliest of the mountaintop residents to go to sleep for the winter. The 28th of August was the last time they saw the light of day, going underground for a nine-month-long nap in the burrow they made two months of improvements on. Forty feet beneath my feet is the summer's excavation site, about a 4x4-foot mound of sandy soil they shoved out of their hole. I can't quite figure out why they go underground so early. They miss the best of Indian Summer.

Thunder in the distance. A smoke report comes across the airwaves from Carey Dome Lookout, a firetower beyond the Salmon River, far to my south. The storm is being born.

The wind picks up. Gusts of twenty miles per hour reach the mountaintop, rustling my journal pages. Time to put the pen down and concentrate on watching the dark southern sky.

I watch the clouds drift off to the northwest, moving away from our District boundary like some sort of anti-polarity pushing them away. The storm season is waning. Unless this black bank of clouds makes a major course change, I'm out of luck to see any more lightning from my alpine nest.

My mountaintop silence is over as I hear a plane overhead going southeast. The terrorist bombing canceled all domestic flights. I never before have seen the sky without any contrails. It's been like a nationwide moment of silence of jet engines.

1600 hours   My best Idaho friend and lookout comrade, Kris Anderson, shows up, putting a huge smile on my face. We embrace at the foot of the stairs and revel at the reunion, which I find out, will only last two hours. Kris and Bob Anderson were our lookout neighbors for years in the 1970s and 1980s at Coolwater Lookout. Bob eventually got a job with the Idaho Transportation Department, but Kris remained a lookout for twenty-eight years. Now she too had retired from her last mountaintop perch at Beaver Ridge to become a nurse. Her day off was today. My lucky day...to see my special friend.

Kris soaked up the only two hours she'd have on lookout this summer as we caught up on what had been going on in our lives. It was the fastest two hours I had spent with someone and she was too soon saying goodbye and heading back down the long and steep lookout road to the Selway and back to Lewiston.

Kris brought me luck. Soon after she left, the biggest storm I had seen this summer was happening northeast of me, thirty miles away, still in my seen area. Every minute three or four strikes would stab at the mountainsides. I faithfully recorded each strike in my lightning-strike record. Guy Williams, the dispatcher, was glad to finally receive a report of lightning hitting our District instead of just missing it. Within twenty minutes the storm stopped its barrage on the forest and dissipated. A rainbow formed in its wake. In the morning I'd be glassing the mountains for any sign of smoke.

🐝 *September 14th* Day 76

0700 hours   I woke throughout the night, checking my northeastern horizon for any orange glows. Nothing. Just the star-studded sky...the crescent moon and Venus taking center stage.

But now I'm up and going, scanning the country through binoculars and...wait—something that shouldn't be there! Something that yes, could be a smoke! I'm all alone. No hurry in the world, but I'm suddenly filled with fear, excitement and about as much tension as the times I stood in front of my high-school-speech class. "Fire!" I yell to nobody. Number two of the year and it's all mine! Shissler Lookout, normally staffed this time of year, hasn't a soul on board. I made a tripod out of my catwalk-perch viewing spot, placing my elbows on the railing, with the 10x42 Cabelas against my eyes. I'm not seeing the drift smoke yet. I need that to conclude it's not just a clearing in the mountainside that appears like smoke.

Pretty soon I see it...movement. Another clue that it is a real smoke. But there are some waterdogs out there also; little puffs of water vapor that can look suspiciously like smoke. Still not a hundred percent sure. But then, a drift line of smoke forms across the mountainside. This is the real McCoy!

I quickly make my way back inside my living area-turned-office and aim my firefinder at the distant smoke. 54 degrees. Off my firefinder map, I run the azimuth line out on my ceiling map and try to figure out where along that line it's coming from. A pure guess. The country east of Shissler Lookout is filled with smoke haze from larger fires to the west. I can't make out the ridgelines right now to get an accurate location.

So I guesstimate the fire's location and call it into Fenn Dispatch. Guy, who sat patiently waiting for a fire all summer long, sounds like he just won the million-dollar lottery, as I announce that I have a smoke to report. Reading off the fifteen details of my second smoke of the season, I well up with pride...that John, the fire spotter, was finally finding what he was being paid to find.

Air Patrol discovers three more smokes to bring the total to four new fire starts from yesterday evening's storm. A regular fire bust. Nearly doubling the District's fire count for the season. Doubling my season total to two.

A fly buzzes by. Another one does a tour around my head. Grasshoppers fling around at the base of the tower, potential gray jay food. A nuthatch *na na na's* down by the outhouse. A northeast breeze sweeps across the treetops out of Bluff Creek, making the familiar water-rushing sound. A Cessna's peaceful drone comes from the Selway Canyon to my north.

All is well on Indian Hill.

🐝 *September 15th Day 77*

    The picture-perfect celestial scene of a crescent moon and Venus, lying just above the Bitterroot Divide, kept me awake before morning light. Shortly after getting back to sleep I was abruptly wakened by the sharp crack of a rifle shot. Opening day of hunting season. And somebody got one of the elk, deer or bears I'd been seeing all summer.

    Too early to start looking for fires, but too late to stay sacked in, I get up and start coffee heating on the stove. Then it's back to listening for other mountaintop morning sounds. But there aren't any. It was Indian Summer quiet. Not a nuthatch, chickadee or gray jay.

    Soon the coffee begins percolating, erasing the silence. The morning routine is started, the coffee aroma filling my humble abode.

    "Williams Peak, this is Sheepeater Lookout," the discreet-channel chat line broke the airwaves.

    "Sheepeater, this is Williams Peak. How do you copy?"

    I leaned over and turned up the volume.

    "I copy you loud and clear," replied Rene, the sixteen-year veteran of one of the most isolated lookouts in the area.

    "Well, I'm just about ready to go. Just a little more cleaning and I'll be ready to head out!" Lily, the first year lookout on the Payette Forest announced.

    "It sure has been good working with you this summer, Lily, and I know others would sure like to see you come back next summer!"

    "Thanks Rene. I sure want to come back. This is such a special place up here! There are just so many hiking opportunities from the lookout. That trail down into Sheep

Creek to the South Fork of the Salmon sure is a special place. I love living in the outdoors and this is such a great place to do it!"

I stayed glued to the airwaves as I had all summer long, eavesdropping into the happenings of the lookouts far to my south. I wished Lily well, even though she didn't hear it, staying stealth to the conversation, listening, but not contributing to the Channel 13 chat. The voices from the Payette Forest Lookouts warmed many a day over the years and especially this year. Mark on War Eagle, Rene on Sheepeater, Charles on Pilot Peak and Lily on Williams Peak—I feel a unique bond with each one of them. Like the leaves of autumn, the lookouts are falling, one by one, scattering to the winds of their civilized futures. Left are my other mountaintop friends, Jay on Gardiner Peak, Bill on Coolwater, Wendy on Sheephill, Donna on Oregon Butte, Dutcher on Pilot Knob, Rusty on Black Mountain, Steve on Bear Mountain, Kelly on Osier Ridge, Esther on Rocky Point and Tanna on Beaver Ridge. But the voice of Williams Peak will be missed a lot…a lookout leaving her beloved mountaintop home.

Goodbye Lily. And good luck in that world below.

🌿 *September 16th Day 78*

0730 hours The morning show has already begun as I lift my chair out of my little glass house and set it on the east side of the catwalk. The rushing sounds of Meadow Creek fade in and out with the whims of the winds, louder then softer—repeating the process over and over. At times the creek seems like it's just below the lookout, but in reality it's a good two air-miles away. The gray jays are perched on the rocks and small fir tree branches below the tower, acting like they're looking for grasshoppers, but I know they're expecting a handout. Their lucky day. I break down and break off a piece of my homemade bread for my buddies. I peer down over the railing's edge and scope out the scene. At least six jays are waiting patiently for the airdrop. I give the bread a good toss over the railing; the light westerly breeze arcing it to the east and the rock wall that circles the tower. Six birds compete for the prize, the lucky one chirping out his excitement as he flies off to stash it in a nearby tree. Five more small sections of the all-grain bread go flying, all my gray jay pets satisfied. They fly off to their treetop caches and I go back to the other morning show. A raven cackles and caws as he circles over the firetower. I feel a communication of sorts as I do my awful impression of one of his own. He caws back, then perches in the top of an old lodgepole tree that stands next to the log cabin, checking out his...our area. A woodpecker beats his brains out against a nearby snag, looking for an early morning larvae meal. An unidentified bird flies by, landing in the top of an alpine-fir tree to the southwest of the lookout tower. He chirps a while, then takes off to parts unknown. One of the gray jays returns, flying past me, then does a graceful ninety-degree turn, lighting on the outside edge of my overhead south-side shutter. He hop-steps his way closer to me, then peers over the edge. Our eyes meet. I encourage him, doing my gray jay imitation. He responds and jumps, diving off the shutter, doing a few quick twists and turns, perching on the railing three feet from me. Out of bread, so out of luck, he dives off the railing and joins the rest of the two jay clans down the road, past the log cabin.

    The radio comes alive from inside my glass house—Pilot Peak Lookout describing to Sheepeater Lookout about the storm that passed in the night. I saw the flashes and now could hear the details of what happened far off to my south after I went to sleep. Lightning hit their section of the Idaho forest quite hard. But the rain with it squelched most of their concern about fires. So far all that could be seen were waterdogs, smoke-looking puffs of moisture that were rising out of the valleys.

I get on the Forest Service radio after catching up on the latest lookout news and check in to Fenn Dispatch, describing what I can see of the Wilderness Fire-Use fires.

Then I go back to the deck and scan the portion of the Selway Bitterroot Wilderness that got hit the hardest in that September 13th storm. Nothing new stares back at me through the 10x42s. I set the binoculars down and look out over the railing like it's a ship's rail...peering down to the rocky reefs forty-one feet below. A chipmunk scampers. A stellar jay looks for grasshoppers. A butterfly flutters by. The morning lookout show is as always...a peaceful way to start the day.

1400 hours   The September sky looks more like a July sky. Towering cumulus are forming a horseshoe-shaped arc of clouds over the eastern portion of our District. The low rumble of thunder can be heard in the distance, just audible over the sound of the northwest breezes.

I watch the cauliflower-edged clouds continue to grow, the tops forming into huge animal-head shapes. A pig's head, complete with snout and ears out of the cloud over Lost Horse Pass. A large ram's head, complete with a large curled rack out of the cloud at the head of East Moose Creek. A shark's head, complete with dorsal fin out over McConnell Mountain.

The thunder is getting louder. Transparent veils of rain angle out of the clouds, disappearing into thin air. Virga. No rain touching the ground. Dry lightning...the most dangerous kind. But still no fire-starting bright flashes out of the heavens.

The animal shapes turn into impressive anvil-shaped clouds. Fifty miles long. Thirty-thousand feet high. Almost continual thunder now. But I'm still not seeing any lightning. My fingers are crossed...addicted to the excitement of watching the storms. I wait patiently for the storm to start stabbing at the Earth, my eyes focusing on the mountain slopes beneath the most impressive clouds of summer.

Sitting back on the catwalk, waiting for the lightning storm, I casually reach up and grab hold of the southeast corner solid copper lightning wire. If the tower got struck now I'd be cooked, fried at the stake. I tempt fate, at ease with the storm's edge a good thirty miles away.

2000 hours   Another storm hits the west side of the District, dropping down strikes in my immediate area. Several forest fire glows can be seen from my perch, but not large enough to warrant fire crews chasing them after dark.

2100 hours   I go out on the west-side catwalk after the storm, and watch the candle-like glows emanating from the jet-black sky. Wind from the dying storm eerily whistles around and through the shutters over my head.

I return inside my glass-walled nest and turn the red-handled crank on the side of the Coleman lantern, slipping in between the cold Forest Service issue sheets. The dying light flickers and goes out, the bright star above the Selway Valley disappearing from the nighttime sky.

🐝 September 17th Day 79

I can't wait until the official 0600 hours start-up time and hop out of bed with the first light of dawn. The jagged crest of the Bitterroot Divide corrals the rest of the unseen country. It's too dark to start scanning for fires, but sleeping wasn't an option.

0540 hours   I had heard a radio squelch earlier. I was guessing that it was Penny Keck, my boss, waking her lookouts.

I was ready. Fire reports and lightning strike records on the varnished knotty-pine table. Pencils sharpened. Ceiling map hinged down for easy reference. Bed made. Coffee perking. Rain measurement recorded. All I needed now was more daylight and little residues of blue appearing out of the thick wrinkled carpet of green.

 0550 hours My first smoke appears. I go into action, lining up the Osborne Firefinder on my fourth fire of the season. Excitement percolates in me like the coffee on the stove. I zero in on the little column and record the azimuth. Then I pinpoint the fire on the map, recording it on the official fire report form. Size, color, drift, rate of spread, time lightning strike occurred. Recorded. I knew Penny was waiting.

 "Fenn, this is Indian Hill," I announced over the airwaves at exactly 0600 hours.

 "Indian Hill, Fenn." Penny must have been holding onto the microphone.

 "Yeah, I've got a smoke coming up just below SOB Ridge."

 "Ready to copy." Penny was all business.

 Fire report number five for the summer came an hour later. Tucked in under a ridge to my northeast was a small plume of smoke. Hard to see, thirty miles away, but not to the spying eyes of a lookout with twenty-eight years of experience.

 1600 hours I scan the mountains for fire number six. But the country looks the way it has most of the summer...fire free. The encore performance of the fire-starting cumulus hasn't happened, the last of the cauliflower-edged clouds dissipating, heading east out of my area. I sense that this might be the beginning of the end to the fire lookout season.

 Sadness wells up inside me as I watch the last of summer float away.

🐝 September 18th Day 80

0830 hours   Everything's back to normal. A gray jay cries for a handout from the top of a nearby fir tree. Swallows use the tower for more bombing runs, veering off at the last moment for another daredevil try at the game of who can come the closest. I duck from the winner of the contest, the little flutter of flight just missing me. Then magically he disappears to parts unknown. I throw out a section of pancake, breakfast leftovers. My airborne gray jay pet does a few dips and weaves to the ground to retrieve the heavenly-dropped morsel. A sparrow hawk flies over the clearing to the north of the tower, checking for movement of his breakfast scurrying along the ground. No movement. He continues on.

My food supply is dwindling. Out of milk, eggs, butter, fresh fruit and vegetables. Low on everything else. Will I make it to the end of the lookout season, which is determined by the cold Alaskan Low that blankets the ridgetop with eight inches of snow? Only with my skill at stretching things to the maximum, adding this to that in every conceivable way, will I make it. Hard tack is my last option, mixing flour and water and letting it dry...like the hard-core army recruits ate in the 1800s. I still had leftover backpack dehydrated food to back me up. Then there were the MRE's. If the Meals Ready to Eat were good enough for the military and fire crews, they were good enough for me.

A large column of black-as-night smoke shoots up like an atomic bomb blast, coming from a wheat field stubble burn on the Camas Prairie to my west. Nothing to concern myself with. It's "controlled", unless the wind picks up and the farmer burns his neighbor's house down.

After a quick check for any forest fires, my vision is drawn back to the Selway Crags and its bare-backed rocky spines and talus-shaped basins. The colors are getting more vibrant, the deepening fall shadows more distinct. I follow the route I took to meet Betsy and Lee, my Coolwater neighbors back in July. I imagine being back on Fenn Mountain again, the highest point in the Crags, giving hugs and high fives to the other summit-team members. The Crags Rendezvous has happened three times with Coolwater. I'm already planning my route to North Three Links Lakes, next year's rendezvous destination.

1200 hours   I always wondered why I felt such a unique bond with my Dad. I lean over the southwest-corner railing, peering out…yes, like I'm looking out over a ship's rail, like my Dad's old sailboat bowsprit…feeling the wind in my face, staring down at the "seas". It was a connection that I could never quite put together, never quite make sense of. But now it all made sense, as a sudden gust of wind swayed the tower like it just hit a sudden ocean swell. We were on two ships. Completely different mediums. But, in a way, similar feelings. I "saw" Dad out there on Lake Michigan, putting his boat on auto pilot and making his way to the bowsprit. I "saw" him peering down at the seas, feeling the boat rhythmically going up and down to the cadence of the swells. I lean over the railing as far as I dare, feeling what my Dad felt out on Lake Michigan, riding the wind swells of my own that pulsate out of the west. A feeling of freedom I know now that we both have locked deep in our souls.

1230 hours   "Indian Hill, Keck!" Penny calls with the sound of urgency in her voice.

I rush around the west and north sides of the lookout, reentering my office in the sky. "Keck, Indian Hill."

"Answer on channel 14!" That sense of urgency again.

I quick switch to the secondary channel. "Keck, Indian Hill."

"We've got a situation up here where a certain individual has quit and headed out cross-country for the Selway! I'd like you to get ahold of somebody at Fenn, using your cell phone, and try to have them intercept this individual when he gets out to the road."

"Ah...okay. I'll tell Fenn dispatch!" I answered as casually as I could.

"Thanks, John. Keck."

"KCO 693." My official call sign number terminated the conversation.

Immediately I got out the bag cell phone and forwarded the sketchy details to Fenn. I could tell that they had as many questions about this situation as I had. But they said they'd send somebody out to look for this individual.

Better than any of the mystery novels I had read this summer. More exciting than a football game between the Green Bay Packers and Chicago Bears. This was big-time stuff for any of the prying lookouts that were scanning channel 14. Who was this individual? Why'd he quit? How'd they know he headed for the river? The questions in my mind mounted. But I couldn't figure out why anyone would quit on Penny Keck. She demanded that her crew have a good work ethic. She might even yell at you if you were working too slow or weren't doing the job good enough. But she had a heart of gold. She'd do anything for her crew. She was known to hike up to thirty miles to deliver fruit and other goodies to her trail crews. Heck, she also brought up steaks, and all the fixings, to Judy and I at the lookout. Yes, I couldn't imagine a person quitting with Penny as their boss.

Constant afternoon scanning for forest fires was my remedy for an excess of nervous energy. Hour four of my vigil for holdover fires or signal fires from the employee who went AWOL, news came that John, the Selway River Campground ranger, was returning to Fenn with one passenger. That was code that they had found him. I still didn't have a clue who it was who'd hiked over some of the roughest terrain on the District and why he quit the job.

Case more or less solved. I could sense a lot of wondering lookout minds about what really happened out there on the job site.

1520 hours   Watching a pair of ravens fly by to the west, I do a redtail-hawk imitation to get their attention. It works. One of them is lured my way to check me out. He does a few loops and rolls and nonchalantly stares at me, watching to see a redtail come flying after him. Seeing the Indian Hill hawk imposter, he swoops up to meet his buddy. Better than the Blue Angels, they do synchronized loops and rolls. One pulls out of formation and does a full three-sixty roll, entertaining his lookout audience.

Life is back to normal at Indian Hill.

September 20th Day 82

1100 hours   It's 52 degrees. Clear skies. Light breeze. The mountains are wearing fall's colorful coat. A perfect day for hiking. And that's what I'm doing, psychologically. A visual trek out across the divide between the Selway River and Meadow Creek drainages, joining my friend Kimberly and her friends Matt and Rob, who just left the lookout ridge on a sixty-mile hike to Paradise. My days off and the weather determine my hikes, limiting my journeys into the backcountry to a maximum of two days. This trip is a four to five day trek, the reason I'm following them in my mind and not my body.

Soon I'll see a mirror flash at the Copper Ridge junction, four miles into their expedition into the heart of the Selway Bitterroot Wilderness. I sit here and wait for the three wilderness wanderers, envious…jealous as heck that they will go beyond my farthest trek east of the lookout ridge for the season.

An orange hunting vest appears through my binocular lens. Kimberly. I put the magnifying lens down and use my signal mirror to flash the ridge two air miles away. No response. Then I do it some more. After my arm gets about ready to fall off, I give up, figuring that they don't have a good enough sun angle for a flash back.

A half hour later their lunch stop is over and the orange vest disappears behind the south flank of Copper Butte, the last contact I'll have with Kimberly.

A couple more fire lookouts announce their departure from the mountaintops. From the count of twenty-three during the height of summer, there are only sixteen left that I can hear over the airwaves. Sadness takes hold of me as the day draws near when I will have to follow the other lookouts' lead, reentering civilization after a pleasant three months away.

1600 hours   Fire number six appears as I do another scan of the mountainsides to the west of the tower. Twenty miles away, barely detectable through binoculars. But definitely a smoke. Bill on Coolwater Lookout confirms what I'm seeing and gives me a cross azimuth to the fire.

I radio in the coordinates to Fenn Dispatch and breathe a sigh of relief that I've officially caught up to last year's fire total.

Job security.

🐝 September 21st Day 83

0830 hours   The attack bomber swallows are at it again, doing strafing runs on the tower, the usual kamikaze pilots bringing reinforcements. It looks like about a hundred are putting Indian Hill into their sights. It's the usual morning's entertainment, watching to see them come as close as they dare before making a splat mark on the railing. It's just a game...I think.

Smoke from Wilderness-Use fires on the eastern portion of our nearly million-acre district fills the lower part of the Moose Creek and Selway River Canyons, like a thousand campfires going all at once. The pale-blue bowl of a sky is filled with mid-and-high-level clouds, with occasional angel-hair veils of moisture hanging off the bottom of the milky-white ceiling.

The swallows are inching their way closer to me on every strafing run, the whooshing of their wings the only sound of the otherwise silent attacks. Chirping now, I sense they are nearing the end to another game of lookout tag.

Within a few minutes my senses prove correct. They disappear from the mountaintop for another twenty-four hours. Where do they go, I don't know.

Alone again.

Another mountaintop voice disappears from the airwaves. Another piece of the orchestral movement that makes lookout life so special. One less instrument to the mountaintop symphony of sounds...the lookout voices, the birds' singing, the rushing sounds of Meadow Creek, the whistling of the wind through the shutters, the buzzing of the bees, the flapping of the flag, the cry of the redtail, the bugling of the elk.

1220 hours   Rarely do I ever get this way, but I'm lonely. Judy sure seems a lot farther than just beyond the Bitterroot Mountains that I can see on my distant east horizon. My parents are a lot farther away—1800 miles—and it feels like it today. Dale and Martin, hunters who camp along the lookout ridge, just left to return to California. Even my gray jay buddies haven't shown up so far today. Yes...quite lonely.

1700 hours Stew is simmering on the stove. It is the last of the meat that I jammed into the midget-sized freezer two months ago. From now on I'll have to ration my remaining supplies. Thanks to hunters, I have potatoes to add to the bubbling brew and fresh peaches for dessert. I'll be eating well for the next couple of days.

September 23rd Day 85

1700 hours I notice a large bird diving off the lookout roof. Too late to grab my camera, I just watch, mesmerized by the awesome beauty of what I soon determine to be an osprey. The second landing on the lookout roof this season, I wonder if he's figuring on moving up from his usual haunt on the Selway River. I can read his mind now..."That lookout tower would sure be the ultimate nesting spot!"

Sorry Mr. Osprey...this spot is taken!

September 24th Day 86

Fall winds are breathing down on the ridgetop, rustling the cured-out sorrel, arcing the limber tops of the alpine fir trees that dot the five-acre lookout clearing. I sit just barely in the wind shadow on the sunny east side. Only an occasional breeze bends around the lookout wind deflector, making me feel its presence.

No contrails this morning. Since the September 11th tragedy there's only been a couple of days when the skies looked like giant tic-tac-toe games of jet exhaust. Today only a few high cirrus have formed into delicate looking milky-white peacock feathers.

🐝 September 25th Day 87

1100 hours   Summer is meeting fall head on, the collision of two seasons about to happen over the lookout ridge. There's a weather alert for strong southerly winds and dry thunderstorms to develop. The winds have already developed, making it hard to write, my notebook pages flapping like a hundred little white flags, fluttering in the nearly constant breeze. To my east the leftovers of the wispy-waved cirrus clouds are quickly getting out of the way for the low pressure cumulus clouds that are marching this way.

The mountains are becoming a giant patchwork quilt of red, orange, yellow and green vegetation. Fall at its best. But as the vegetation is dying, so is the lookout season. And my thoughts once again return to once more going back to civilization. I look forward to being with my best friend Judy again at our Montana home. Friends and family. Milkshakes, movies and showers. But every yearly migration back to the "other world" gets more difficult. Lookout life is totally the opposite of what's in store for me in civilization. Life on the mountaintop is simple, structured and comfortable. Life on the "outside" is complicated, structureless and at times quite uncomfortable. The votes in my mind add up to staying rather than leaving my paradise on Indian Hill. Just send up a couple-hundred books, food for nine months, a few cords of firewood, and plenty of notebook paper to write my thoughts and I'd be happy. John...the all-year-round-mountaintop hermit. Yeah, I like the sound of that.

But reality's facing me and soon that cold Alaskan Low will move inland, snuffing out the wilderness fires that keep puffing away. And then it will be over...my turn to deal with life down below.

Channel 14 chat-line gossip fills the lookout room with the voices of Bear Mountain and Rocky Point. I put down the pen and listen closely to the fire description bits and pieces of information, putting enough together to become concerned about Judy and our Lolo Creek house that could be in jeopardy. I look up and see the large cumulus cloud of smoke on my far northeastern horizon. But how far northeast? Lolo Creek by chance? I rush inside and grab the microphone, waiting patiently for the lookouts to clear themselves from the airwaves. Then a lull in talk and I jump in…"Bear Mountain, Indian Hill."

"Indian Hill, Bear Mountain."

"Yeah, Steve, I was overhearing Rocky Point and yourself talking about a large fire over in Montana." I tried to stay calm and not let the panic come across in my voice. "I'm quite concerned because we have a house over in Lolo Creek!" The panic was exposed.

"We're trying to figure out where it's coming from too. Right now we think it's a ways beyond Lolo Creek. My azimuth is 51 degrees, 20 minutes. Esther's is 52 degrees."

"I copied, Steve. Keep me updated when you hear something!"

My rational mind said I didn't need to worry. Two fairly far apart lookouts getting similar bearings to the fire. That would mean the fire is a long ways away from them. Two fairly different readings would be a reason for concern. But until I got confirmation from Bear Mountain Lookout that all was well up Lolo Creek, I was worried sick! My wait for Steve's return call brought out the maps that included Lolo Creek and Rocky and Bear Mountain Lookouts. I laid them on the bed and ran out 52 degrees from Bear Mountain. The azimuth crossed a safe distance from our Lolo Creek house. Then Rocky Point's azimuth told the same story. I started breathing a sigh of relief.

"Indian Hill, Bear Mountain," Steve's voice echoed off my glass-walled house.

"Bear Mountain, Indian Hill."

"The fire's out by Seeley Lake! So it looks like things are safe up Lolo Creek!"

"Well, thanks for the update, Steve!"

"Any time, John. Bear Mountain."

"Indian Hill."

My mind was finally put at ease. But as I looked out at the solid timber that covered the mountainside to my west and remembered the thick timber at the Lolo Creek house, I knew that someday we might be running for our lives from a raging forest fire.

September 27th Day 89

1320 hours I wipe the last of the Camas Prairie dust from my windows, enjoying my crystal clear million-acre view. Put the shutters down and I couldn't stay up here for fifteen minutes. Put the shutters up and I've made it twenty-eight years. The dust from the wheat fields that have been burned over, the exposed soil picked up and pasted on my windows with the wind-driven rain from out of the west is finally removed from my view.

Smoke from the wilderness fires fills the valley floors. If you're at or below 4,000 feet, you're breathing smoke. At 6,810 foot elevation plus 41 feet for the tower, you're out of the smoke, and loving life. I feel bad for the fire crews having to breathe the ugly gray brew of burning residue. But unfortunately that's one of the hazards of their job.

Yesterday's resupply couldn't have been timed better. When the MRE's started to look tempting, I knew I was in trouble. My thanks go out to the gracious outfitter, Sherry Nygard, who bought the supplies. And thanks to Jaycee Nygard who brought the supplies. And thanks to Darrin who called Sherry about the supplies. Thanks to Virginia who mailed my letters. Thanks to Rich who gave me the peaches. Thanks to Cheryl and Marvin for the four delicious dinners. Thanks to Penny who brought me the steak, melon and mail. Aw, heck...thanks to everybody who has helped me through another year on Indian Hill!

Clearings, rocks, brush, snowbanks in the early summer. False smokes. Things that look like smoke but aren't. After nearly three decades up here looking for fires, I've got them all memorized. Until fall, when the yellows of the brush and larch trees are getting too numerous to know from memory. Every new brush or tree color change I check out again. And again and again and again.

🐝 *September 28th Day 90*

1140 hours   Fenn Mountain looks like an island in the Pacific, the 8,021-foot-high peak north of me, pushing through the ocean of fog that surrounds it. Indian Hill is barely in the clear, the fog level settling like a soft cushion of water lapping at the shores of the tree-covered ridge below me. My thoughts drift off again to my Dad and his old sailboat, casting out into the waters of Lake Michigan. The tower stands at the edge of what looks like could be navigated...floated upon to get to Fenn Mountain. My "ship", though stays stationary with the no-wind status, while I "see" my Dad's teakwood-trimmed fiberglass sailboat going out of the Milwaukee harbor, swaying with the wind swells, bobbing up and down with the water swells.

1200 hours   A peaceful ocean of fog now surrounds me, the thick misty gray moisture locking the tower in its grip.

1400 hours   The fog thickens, the wind whipping the grayish brew around the tower. I "see" my Dad again, his boat separated from shore by a thick Lake Michigan fog bank, the lonely, isolated feeling taking hold of him as he listens to the fog horn coming from the invisible Milwaukee harbor. I see him struggling to locate himself, to discover a way safely back to shore. He decides to drop sail and wait, listening for a passing ship, waiting for the outline of the phantom barge to suddenly appear, its bow cutting through the waves and the fog, heading straight for him.

September 29th Day 91

Indian summer returns from a brief retreat, after giving way to the fog, cold and wind of yesterday. Today there's a big bowl of blue sky above me. It's that fall quiet—no wind. Only a couple of flies buzz around my head. I take a swipe at one, but miss.

Wilderness Use "let-burn" fires are peaceably smoking away, columns of gray-blue smoke from the Selway canyon to my northeast, my lookout season "extenders" consuming more grass, brush and trees.

Nothing to do but to watch for new smokes and read the two-year-old newspaper I found in the burn box in the corner of the room.

2050 hours   A long, drawn out scream echoes up from the canyon to my east, followed by another blood-curdling message that a cougar is lurking below. Rarely do I ever get scared up here. I close the trapdoor gate. Tonight I'm scared.

🐝 October 1st Day 93

1600 hours   Red smoke on the Selway. The "let-burn" wilderness fires are getting bigger as the wind fans the flames east. I'm fifteen miles southwest of the closest column of the thick dark gray residue of burning grass, brush and trees. Feeling safe. Shissler Lookout is two air miles from the flames. Luck would have it that Tom, the Lookout, left for school in August. The little white building on the mountaintop to my northeast is in the fire's path—days or weeks away. The only thing that can save it is the weather…the end of the fire season snowstorm that will put the fire out.

🐝 October 3rd Day 95

1600 hours   The wind has a different sound to it. A different feel. No more is it that warm breeze out of the southwest. Now it's louder. Stronger. And colder. Out of the northwest, the first of a series of cold Alaskan air is blowing across the mountaintop. The whistling through the shutters is singing a new tune. Indian Summer is leaving and the cold bite of winter is on its way.

🐝 October 4th Day 96

0830 hours   Life's different since the September 11th terrorist attacks. I look at every contrail, watching for erratic flying behavior. I duck when a Cessna zooms over the tower.

My gray-white companion flutters up to perch on the railing

to get fed. "Hey little buddy! Wanna get fed?" He looks so soft, so cuddly, so dang pettable. He cocks his head sideways, trying to encrypt the human code. I put a piece of wheat bread in my hand and hold the offering at chest height to my fluffed-out companion. He straightens, his eyes aglow for what he knows is food. He hops off the railing and flies into the hand of man. He quickly grabs the bread and feigns a dive over the catwalk. Then he turns his head, the black, beady eyes looking up at me with the look of trust. He turns his head back to the forty-one-foot drop off, then returns to stare at me. "You are so cute…" Another look over the edge of my world and off he flies, gracefully gliding between the trees, crying out his excitement.

I go back to washing the windows of Camas Prairie dust again, the wonderful bond of bird and man touching the inner depths of my soul.

1830 hours The sun casts an eerie orange glow through the smoke-filled sky as I follow the southwest ridge off Indian Hill to my spring. I hike along the narrow ribbon of a trail through well-placed sticks and logs funneling me onto the main water path, keeping me from veering off on the deer and elk trails that braid the lookout ridge.

I had worked the trail all summer, cutting out windfalls and brush, exposing the tread I followed every other night. It was a loop-trip hike, the southwest ridge trail that led to the meadow trail that led to the woods trail and the final descent to the spring on the road. During the early part of the season I'd just get my water from the upper spring that lay hidden to all but the most observant. Tonight I was going to the lower spring, the dripping status of the secret spring too slow for any serious attempt at getting water.

Soon I was at the top of the grassy opening, looking out over what had earlier been a mountainside filled with orange, red, purple, yellow and white wildflowers bobbing up and down in the slightest of breezes. A red ball of a sun sank behind Iron Mountain, the dying light reflected off the golden-grasses of the high mountainslope.

I soaked up the last of the rays and went on my way, switchbacking to the bottom of the twenty-acre opening in the thick carpet of trees.

For years the meadow trail portion of the two-mile round trip water trail was a mystery. I figured there had to be a path connecting the southwest ridge tread with the ravine-route tread. But no matter how much trampling around I did on the steep mountainside, I couldn't find it. Then one day I did see it! Not from the meadow, but from a narrow opening in the trees along the road, above the trailhead. Sure enough, the trail stood out like I had never seen it before, making a big Z in the grassy slope.

The bottom of the Z led me into a wooded ravine, then out into a series of openings that ushered me to the horse water trough along the Indian Hill road.

It was a special spot. Tucked beneath a ridge it held memories of a lot of summers on the lookout. It was the cool amongst the hot. The perennial wet amongst the dry. Sub-alpine fir trees stood like sentries guarding the spring, their perfectly shaped spires shadowing over the effervescent flow of water.

I put down the backpack and connected a white pipe to the black pipe that fed water to the trough. Water slowly made its way past the hollowed-out log, cascading to the board I used as a platform for the half-gallon milk jugs. Three minutes a fill-up, this slow time of year. Time to wander, to check out the animal tracks, the dried-up flowers, the aspen trees. A slight wind whisper turned the leaves of autumn into thousands of tiny hands all clapping at once, the soothing sound blending with the trickling sounds of water.

Water bottles filled, backpack on, I headed back through the dying remnants of summer, the rusty red sorrel, the yellow false huckleberry and the orange mountain ash berries brushing my legs. I switchbacked my way to the upper spring, stopping to listen for the sound of life. An occasional drip from the hidden water source was all I heard.

Up through the huckleberry brush, making my way to the lodgepole thicket that takes me into the fir-and-spruce ravine that I pass through at the bottom of the meadow-switchback trail. Another couple switchbacks and I intersect with the southwest ridge, following it to the road to the south of the tower.

I look up at my home, the little white building atop the tower that stands on a rocky knob. Nearly three decades of feelings suddenly surface, memories of the past when I'd return from my waterhauls and see Judy looking out over the railing for me like a ship captain's wife standing watch for her husband's return from sea. I miss her. I missed the woman who'd wave when I crested the ridge with our ration of water. Her Johnny coming home.

I continued to the lookout, nobody to wave to. Nobody to hug when I got home.

October 5th Day 97

0745 hours "Indian Hill, Fenn." Bill Wilkinson's voice shot like a bullet into the room. I was hit by the words like I'd been wounded. I knew that this radio call could be my one-way ticket out of here.

Hesitant, I picked up the microphone that suddenly seemed dangerous to touch. "Fenn, Indian Hill," I answered meekly, cringing for the reply that I was afraid to hear.

"Yeah Indian Hill. Would you give Dispatch a call on the phone?"

Cell phones. Modern society. Instant private connection to the outside world. I avoided using my new means of communication like a deadly disease. I cleared from the radio waves and picked up the telephone waves. Scared. Terrified that this was it. My last official moments of not knowing when I was being kicked out of my beloved mountaintop nest.

"Hello, Bill speaking!"

"This is Indian Hill." I used my mountain name.

"Yeah, John…what's the weather doing up there?"

"Oh, pretty nice out. Think it frosted this morning."

"Yeah, was thirty-six in Kamiah this morning."

Weather talk turned to hunting talk, questions from my boss about how many hunters were on the mountain. But I knew Bill didn't call to chit chat as he soon got to the real reason he had me call Dispatch.

Like a ton of bricks the words came down on me, crushing my spirits to know I was soon heading back to civilization. Come Monday, Tuesday or Wednesday of next week I'd follow the cold Alaskan Low back to civilization.

I'd look forward to seeing Judy. But how I'd miss my friend in the sky.

1830 hours   My after-hours hike is cut short at the discovery of bear tracks along the Patrol Ridge trail to the south of the lookout. Very big bear tracks that were probably from the nine-foot bear that hunters swore they had seen in the area. My skepticism turned into "true believer" status as the huge impressions in the dusty soil caused me to do a button-hook turn back to the tower.

2000 hours   I started a fire and placed a half-filled porcelain wash basin on the stove for my evening's entertainment. Thinking about it all summer, I finally figured on putting the idea into motion. Taking a bath. The only part of my body that would be in the bath was my butt. Everything else would stay warm from the fire that was roaring with the added sticks of wood stuffed into the firebox.

My finger-dipping temperature gauge told me that I was ready to put my plan into action. I grabbed the blue handles and quickly placed the basin on the shorter of the two glass-insulated lightning stools. Perfect. Now, set the lantern by the stove and remove clothes. Still perfect. Then I slowly sank into the hot tub.

OUUUCCHHHHH! The pan seared the inside of my legs like a branding iron. Needles of pain shot into the back of my thighs. First-degree burns. Burns that reminded me of how stupid it was not to test pan temperature also.

Scrambling for the first-aid kits, I find two. Opening them I find no tape for compress bandages. No burn ointment. No anything to help alleviate the pain that was now getting worse! Then I found first-aid instructions...

Burn Classification

First Degree- The outer skin is

reddened and welted or slightly

swollen.

Bingo! Now I read to find out what to do about it...

Cold Water Treatment

Immerse minor or first-degree

burns in cold water until the

patient ceases to feel pain. Use

ice cubes to keep water so it feels cold to the patient.

Bummer. No ice cubes. And the spring water's been warming all day. I used the next best thing. Frozen huckleberries in a wash cloth, the moistened rag pressed firmly on my reddened flesh. OUCH! Cold stinging on top of hot stinging.

Off and on applications of frozen huckleberry therapy helped. Then the Vaseline on the 4x4 bandage sealed it for the night. My bath experiment a total failure, I fell asleep with the wind rocking the tower like a 41-foot-high cradle.

🐝 October 7th Day 99

0830 hours The Selway is filled with the leftovers of yesterday's wilderness fire run, the grayish blue smoke fingering into the tributaries of Halfway, Meeker, Three Links and Ballinger Creek.

It's a beautiful blue-sky morning. Twenty-three degrees when I woke at 0630, thirty-nine degrees now. A residue of frost still clings to the log cabin roof, the white shingles proof of a damn cold night. A ten blanket damn cold night.

The lookout season is barely holding on, the last of my lookout comrades beginning to show signs of the extended stay on their mountaintops. Rusty on Black Mountain is out of dog food for his furry companion. Kelly on Osier Ridge is nursing an ankle injury. Jay on Gardiner is almost out of food, his last resupply going "over the hill" in a mule-train wreck on the Selway trail. I sit up here, happy as a clam. Resupplied with food, twenty-five gallons of spring water in milk cans on the deck, a good wood supply to kill the October chill. And enough books to last another month.

But one look over my shoulder confirms the season-ending event, the thick line of moisture-filled clouds that is slowly erasing the last of the blue of my Indian Summer morning.

I know it's time to prepare to leave my beloved home. Time to pack away what I brought up here on my first day. Time to wax the floor, clean the stove, and defrost the miniature-sized refrigerator. Shutters on the log cabin windows. Ashes in the outhouse. The routed Indian Hill sign taken down. But the last of the dying summer's warmth feels too good to leave my out-of-the-wind leeward spot on the catwalk. Until that gray makes it my way, I'm sitting here, looking out over the endless wilderness, smelling the fresh scent of fall, listening to the breeze whistling through the shutters, eddying around the corner of my lookout home. A chipmunk rattles the leaf-covered sorrel at the foot of the tower. A pine squirrel chatters from a nearby lodgepole. My soul, my life still is at peace...barely.

Tonight's supper was the official "Indian Hill" birthday supper. A can of Mountain Dew that a lookout visitor left, along with baked chicken, steamed broccoli and fresh out-of-the-can jellied cranberry sauce. Fifty years old, my summer home for the last twenty-eight of those years, I celebrated. And sang Happy Birthday to Indian Hill. I revel in the fact that we were both "born" in the same year.

The rest of the evening I huddled around the heat of the woodstove to offset the deep chill in the air, as wind-blown snow began falling like confetti on the mountaintop.

🌿 *October 8th Day 100*

1115 hours The steady dripping of melting snow off the shutters. The lookout tower encased in a thick sea of fog. I know it's time to pack up and leave my mountaintop home.

Sadness wells up in me as it has the last several days, tears surfacing. I procrastinate a little longer on packing, not yet willing to deal with reality.

1700 hours   I stare out the west-side windows at curtains of white slashing out of the opaque northwest sky. The evergreen spires are instantly frosted, the ground covered with an inch of snow.

I "see" the shutters closing in front of my eyes, sealing me off from the weather, and making a wall where there was none for the last three and a half months. I "feel" the depths of winter from inside the boarded-shut little hut, imagining the storms that will rock the tower upon its footings. But I "see" spring coming, the deep snows of winter finally receding, thunderheads forming over the Selway River valley. Lightning stabbing at the mountainsides. Then I "see" the ground squirrels playing out on the rocks, the gray jays landing on the railing. I "see" myself coming home, with another three months of supplies. I breathe in deep, taking in the fresh alpine scent...the phlox, the beargrass and evergreens blending into a uniquely wonderful aroma. I "see" the shutters opening again, the light entering the nine-month-dark room.

And I feel my spirit once again renewed.

🐝 *October 9th   Day 101*

0700 hours   I feel like I'm in a giant cocoon, my glass walls plastered with more wind-blown snow. It's cold, the heat from the woodstove barely fighting off the frigid air that's ushered through every crack in the meager shield against the wintry gale.

0950 hours   A radio call comes with the words I fear... "We're sending somebody up tomorrow to bring you down!" the Dispatcher announces.

The fog, the cold, the snow. Nothing gives me as desperate a feeling as the word, "Down". Going back down where I came from over three months ago.

I had twenty-four hours left. The clock was ticking on my time on Indian Hill.

1030 hours   A foreign sound to the wind, the gray jays and fire crackling…an engine down by the log cabin. I wipe the inside of the steamed-up window by the playhouse-size refrigerator and peer out through the porthole at Marvin, the local outfitter, his truck running, his head poking out of the rolled-down window. I open the door to a face full of confetti-like snow eddying around and through the entry.

"Hey Marvin!" I yell into the fog, peering out over the railing as much as I dare.

"Hey John!" he yells back. "Ya finding any fires in this stuff?"

"Oh yeah…you bet! I'll catch anything within a hundred yards of the tower!"

"When they packing ya down?" shot Marv's half of the 200-foot conversation to my perch.

"Got the call half an hour ago. They're pulling me down tomorrow! Hey, you want some coffee?"

"Ya don't need to put any on for me." Marv's words filtering through the gray.

"No bother. Just take five minutes to brew up." I think I was looking for someone to talk to.

"I'll be right up!" He must have been looking for someone to talk to too.

Marvin was the closest that a 21st Century person could come to being a 19th Century mountain man. Those rough, tough looks. That walk of confidence. I felt like every time I saw him he looked like he just came out of the woods, which he usually had. Knew every trail in the country, day or night. Nicknamed Midnight Marvin, he rode as much in the dark as he did in the light of day. "Never used a flashlight," he'd say. "Ruins the horse's vision!"

The tower started to shake, rattle and roll as he approached the catwalk entryway. As he broke through the doorway, snow blowing in with my mountaintop neighbor, we shook hands. "How's it going, Marv?"

"Oh fine. Back's been hurtin' a little since that shoeing accident this summer." He half bent over, feeling the spot.

"What happened?" He looked in pain.

"Oh, doggone it!" He straightened. "Ended up getting all tangled up with this here mule. Old Mable didn't take too kindly to being pinched by the handles of those clippers I had hanging from my pocket. She had a fit and knocked me down, then she kicks me in the back and the head. I'll tell you what... that hurt like hell!"

"Gosh, I bet it did!" I grabbed the coffeepot off the stove. "Straight or with creamer?"

"Nice and black for me!" I poured the percolated brew into the Forest Service china cup and handed it to him.

"No permanent damage, I hope!" I poured a cup for myself.

"Felt okay after a while, but then it all of a sudden hurt like hell! Next thing ya know this big old lump formed right on my backbone. Then I lost all the feeling in my legs!"

"That would have freaked me out!"

"It did freak me out!"

"So what happened next?"

"Saw the ol' doc and he found some bone splinters. So he pulled them out. Felt great ever since!"

"Thank goodness it wasn't more serious!"

Back talk turned to hunting talk. Then to the trips into the backcountry we both wanted to take. Cabins we'd build if we could. One yarn led to another until Midnight Marvin got up to go. As he put the coffee cup down and headed for the door, he stopped, turned towards me and said, "Ya know, John, you're my best friend on the mountain. Some day you and me ought to take a trip together into that backcountry. I'll bring the stock. We'll just ride into some of those basins we'd build a log cabin in if it were legal." He opened the door. "Ya know..." He turned and faced me. "Ya ever get an inkling to go, just let me know!"

"Yeah...sounds great, Marv." Our right hands met. "We'll definitely have to do that some day."

He turned and walked away, the spurs from his cowboy boots clinking as he disappeared through the catwalk opening.

2100 hours   A cold blanket of air settles down over the mountaintop. The snow has stopped. But the wind still plays tag with the lookout, feeling its way through the shutters, the whispering breeze singing old familiar tunes.

The last of the dying lantern light casts mirrored impressions in the windowpanes. The chugging sound stops. A last flicker from the glass globe and the lone star above the Selway goes out.

Fritz jumping into the attic off of Judy's back

Mouse house in drawer on opening day in 2007

Supply stash on opening day

Our cat family -- Fritz, Rhoda and Fluffy

Fluffy soaking up the sun

Rhoda napping on the firefinder

Cumulonimbus clouds over the wilderness

Flare-up from a lightning strike

Judy making a cheese cake

Sunrise with valley fog

Much looked forward to family visit in 1998

Downstrikes and cloud-to-cloud lightning

A fire bust on the District

Dad helping plot fires

Family reunion at the lookout

Posing at the firefinder

Keeping busy scraping paint off the windows

3 gallons of huckleberries after days of picking

Making huckleberry pancakes

Lightning fire in Bluff Creek -- 1998

At the lower spring

Water haul with Honda 90

Trying to entice ground squirrels out of their burrows with bread

Storm clouds

Keeping in shape doing chin-ups at the cabin

Tree that fell across the road by the lookout

Smokejumper having bad luck

Helicopter long-lining supplies for fire crew

Black bear below lookout tower

District fire crew coming off a nearby fire in 1994

Hoisting up water container

Penny Keck visiting the lookout

Gray jay eating out of my hand

Mountain goat passing through clearing

A week-long visit in 1983 with my "Little Brother" Carl Johnston from the Big Brothers and Sisters program

Plotting a fire on the firefinder a mile from the lookout

John and Judy in 2007

Clouds lifting after a storm

My adventure buddy Gary Winek at the Trailhead heading into the wilderness in 2005

Replacing rotting west-side windows

New windows that I built installed

Columbian ground squirrels fighting over a pancake

Lining up a fire using the Osborne Firefinder

My attempt at making huckleberry bread

Fenn fire crew

District packer heading into the wilderness

Upper spring

Signaling Coolwater Lookout

Bob and Kris Anderson — the Coolwater Lookouts in the 1970s and 1980s

John and Judy with the Crags in background

Above: A successful elk hunter

Left: Woodstove that I installed in 1994

Fresh snowfall

Season-ending snowfall

Collecting snow to melt for washing dishes

Bear tracks in the snow near tower

Above: Idaho County Sheriff's Department searching for a lost hunter in 2007

Right: Double rainbow in Bluff Creek

Above: Coolwater Ridge covered in snow

Sunset from inside lookout

"No! I don't want to go!"

2003

It was the middle of the night, on July 16th, when what *shouldn't* be happening was happening outside my lookout windows...the Slims Fire on the opposite side of Meadow Creek was exhibiting extreme fire behavior when it should have been lying back down. It was started by lightning my first night on Indian Hill, July 7th, and I reported it to Fenn Dispatch as a flare-up that apparently was "sleeping" the next morning. And it stayed dormant for the next week, coming back to life on the 15th.

Over the years I had seen nothing like it, a lightning-caused fire that *wasn't* quickly contained, controlled and put out in a fairly short order. The Grangeville smokejumpers who dropped on the fire weren't able to contain it as of yet, and it didn't look promising to be put out anytime soon. After making the jumpers aware of the increased fire activity, I tried, but failed to go back to sleep, with one thought plaguing my mind. If the fire ended up crossing over on my side of Meadow Creek I could be running for my life from a raging forest fire! I tossed and turned, each time looking out across Meadow Creek at the 200-foot flames that lit up the nighttime sky.

Journal Notes for July 17th, 2003...

Other lookouts just relaxing enjoying the morning, while I am sitting here worried about what might be developing across the canyon. Lots of fire activity overnight and at least 40 acres are burned already. Erin Law just flew it, and WOW...crews pulling off the mountain and regrouping at Slim's Camp.

And I was "regrouping" up at Indian Hill, realizing that I might only have days left of my lookout season. The height of the flames, the futility of the firefighters' efforts, and the fact that there were thousands and thousands of densely packed evergreen trees on the extremely steep slope below me told me that the end might be near. Echoes of Wick's constant reminders to always keep a close eye on the forest below in Meadow Creek also rang alarm bells.

    Everything about this lookout season so far seemed strange—the fact that the forest *wasn't* as green as it should have been, the fact that I had barely explored the mountaintop before I was essentially stuck on the firetower, glad to be the *eyes* for the smokejumpers, the fact that the snow in the high country had disappeared so early...the sounds of snowmelt cascading off of the steep rock walls of Bluff Creek nonexistent, the vegetation nearly being fall crunchy already when you walked below the tower, dust clouds coming from the roads. But some things remained the same and warmed my heart...the beautiful pink, purple and white carpet of phlox that covered the mountaintop, the ice-cream-cone shaped, yellow beargrass that came in on its heals, the early-morning elk and deer visits as they made their way through the clearing beneath my feet, the grand Montana-to-Oregon 220-mile long view that I woke up to every day, the hawks and the eagles soaring above the lookout ridge, and my gray jay companions coming to my call, flying up to the lookout to eat bread out of my hand, which always made my day.

🌲 *Official journal entries for July 17th...*

Fire is approximately 40 acres. Crews working to complete line. By mid-afternoon fire gets too active to work and crews pull back, seeking safety. Nobody now is working on fire.

1240 hours...Considerable torching going on on west flank of fire. Type II team ordered. Air attack is ordered, along with 2 light tankers from Grangeville. Light helicopter doing bucket drops.

1430 hours...Air Attack discusses with Rocky (Incident Commander for smokejumpers) about best method of attack and they both agree that the current fire behavior calls for a more aggressive strategy and that heavy air tanker and heavy helicopter support is needed to slow the blaze.

1432 hours...Air Attack calls Grangeville Dispatch about ordering heavier air support.

    Early in the morning of the 18th, during a rare lull in the fire activity, I took my hand-held Forest Service radio, and went to get water. I loaded up the two 10-gallon milk cans, several 5-gallon plastic water jugs, and a couple of quart-size canteens in the bed of my Nissan pickup and made my way down the lookout driveway to replenish my supply for the next week. Down past the Copper Butte and Otter Butte Trailheads, then around the hairpin switchback and the start of the Meadow Creek Trail, I arrived at the place that gave me so much peace. I did some Y-turns at the wide spot in the road above the water trough and turned off the ignition and turned on my senses to fully absorb the tranquil setting. Water cascaded out of the log horse trough this early in the season, trickling into the culvert at my feet, forming one of the many branches of Little Creek and its mile-long journey to Meadow Creek. I connected the white PVC pipe to the black pipe that came from the spring to get it to flow over the trough. Then I placed one of the plastic jugs under the strong flow, and while waiting went down to one of my favorite spots on the mountain, where the spring trail from the lookout came out on the road—the site of the only aspen grove on Indian Hill. A slight breeze started up as the aspen leaves sounded like tiny pebbles washing up on shore. I stood there, absorbing the moment, immersed in the beauty of nature's chorale, listening to the aspen music above my head. Then I went back to the watering hole and capped the filled container and placed another one under the spigot, which led to more exploring, this time going up the road to the sound of yet another spring that bubbled up on the downhill side of the road. I jumped off the bank and checked out one of the three springs that I knew of on the mountain. Too slow of a flow to seriously consider getting my water from here, I watched this spring forming the smallest creeklit that began its journey to the deep valley below. Timing the second water fill-up, I made my way back to change water jugs once more, this time walking back up the road to the pearly everlasting that I had seen coming down, resurrecting memories of when Judy would cut bouquets of the white wildflowers to hang upside down from the log cabin loft to dry so she could use them for flower arrangements. The small pearl-shaped flowers were just starting to form, so I'd have to wait to cut some for the woman who I was already missing.

After filling the ten-gallon milk cans, and jamming the water jugs into the bed of the pickup, I headed back up to the lookout. I left the two heavy milk cans on the log cabin porch and yanked the five-gallon jugs up to the top of the tower using the pulley rope.

The Slims Fire wasn't the only fire that started from the lightning storm in the middle of my first night on the lookout. Two other fires; one in Doe Creek to my south, and one in Pinchot Creek, across the Selway to my north-northeast, flared up in that first lightning storm. Doe Creek wasn't showing any more, but Pinchot was showing a very definite column of smoke this morning that I reported to Fenn Dispatch.

🌲 *Official logbook journal notes for July 18th...*

0828 hours...Indian Hill to Nelson   Smoke really picking up south of ridge, down close to Meadow Creek.

1428 hours...Indian Hill to Nelson   West flank of fire making a run—lots of torching along ridge and north of ridge

1445 hours...Nelson to Indian Hill   Does it look like fire will get to the head of the canyon?

Indian Hill to Nelson   Yes, but will go to southwest part of canyon and should not go north.

1450 hours...Nelson to 68-Hotel (light helicopter)   Need bucket drops ASAP

1529 hours...Indian Hill to Nelson   68-Hotel headed your way to do bucket drops

1537 hours...68-Hotel to Indian Hill   At fire site. Will follow local. Relayed to Fenn Dispatch.

1600 hours...Temperature at Fenn Ranger Station got to be 106 degrees. Temperature at Moose Creek got to 110 degrees.

1840 hours...Nelson to Indian Hill   What is the status of the fire?

Indian Hill to Nelson   The fire is very active with a brown/orange based column in southeast quarter. Fire extends from southeast corner down to Meadow Creek I think, but I can't see all the way into the canyon.

1842 hours...Nelson to Indian Hill   Will keep helicopter around till sun gets off slope.

On the morning of July 19th, I gave the following update to Erin Law at Fenn Dispatch...

0715 hours...The fire was very active, with considerable torching until 2030 hours. The southeast and west flanks were the most active parts of the fire. There is strong inversion smoke right now in the north draw. North draw was fairly active last night. The inversion is slowly lifting.

In the afternoon the Lolo Hotshots joined the fire fight, the crew mirror flashing me from their location, which I recorded on my firefinder map with a grease pencil.

On the morning of July 20th, I received the tactical channels for the various fire crews fighting the Slims Fire...

TAC #1...Channel 1   Division Alpha—Ronan 10 and Nez Perce 5

TAC #2...Channel 2   Division Bravo—Idaho Panhandle IHC

TAC #3...Channel 3   Division Pappa—Lolo IHC and Orofino C10

Channel 13   Air to Ground

🌲 *Official journal notes for the 20th...*

0718 hours...Indian Hill to Lolo Hot Shots   Activity increasing in draw—hard to tell if it crossed the creek.

0745 hours...Lolo Hot Shots to Indian Hill   Smoke column in north draw—can't tell if fire crossed the creek.

0821 hours...Indian Hill to Lolo Hot Shots and Orofino Red Hots   Winds 10-15 mph up here.

Fire notes in logbook...Most activity yesterday evening between 2030 and 2100 hours. Fire at 320 acres.

0955 hours...Idaho Panhandle crew to Fenn Dispatch   We have a good smoke coming up out of the south side of the fire.

1220 hours...Indian Hill to Lolo Hot Shots, Orofino Red Hots and Panhandle crew   Winds have increased to 20 mph out of the WNW.

1230 hours...Wilkinson to Indian Hill   What's the fire behavior?

Indian Hill to Wilkinson   There's increasing fire behavior on the south flank, moving south southwest. Winds seem to be affecting fire, but doesn't look like winds are as strong down below.

Up on Indian Hill I was getting more and more worried. Worried about the reports of the fire getting close, if not down at Meadow Creek by now, which was the last fifty-foot wide fire line between the lookout and the Slims Fire. Once it was breached I knew that I could be in trouble. The tower could be in trouble, knowing that the wooden tower would be in the fire's path if it swept up from Meadow Creek to the top of the ridge! The valiant, but failed efforts to control the fire by all the tough-as-nails fire crews led me believe that surely my days were indeed numbered up on lookout for the summer. But, I knew, that I wouldn't ever let my buddy be unprotected from a raging forest fire. I hoped the decision would be made to fire wrap it before that could ever happen. I wouldn't let down my friend in the sky!

Knowing that only a miracle would save my lookout season, I started boxing up the things that were only recently brought up for another three-month stay. Books, clothes, dry goods, canned goods, personal journal, writing paper, and more were thrown in the boxes that I brought up from the log cabin, getting ready for the word to evacuate my summer home. And it didn't look good as I peered out to the west and *saw* my season coming to an end with a breach of Meadow Creek. But I still had a little more time, as that "fire line" was holding for the moment!

I decided that if I had to race out of here from the Slims Fire, that I'd at least have a decent last breakfast at the crack of dawn on the 21st, and a source for some gray jay handouts. So I fried up some of the bacon on the miniature-size stove and mixed up some pancake mix as soon as the sun peeked above the sawtoothed Bitterroot Mountains that formed the divide between Idaho and Montana, a good sixty miles away. I reveled in the fact that this was my 31st year on Indian Hill as I munched on the oh-so-good flapjacks and bacon, washed down with some canned pineapple orange juice from my stash. I gave a toast to the brave and strong fire crews who were working so hard on trying to control the beast that was raging in the canyon to my west. Then, as planned, I saved a last pancake for my gray jay companions and took it out on the east side of the catwalk and gave my best impression of one of their own. Soon I heard one in reply, waiting patiently in a tall alpine fir on the Bluff Creek side, for me to ring the "dinner bell". One more gray jay call and off he swoops from the draping arms of the fir, and flies up to perch on the railing, ten feet from me. "Come on, little buddy, it's a pancake…your favorite!" Then he hop steps his way closer on the three-foot high railing and then into my outstretched hand to get the loot. He pecks at the piece of pancake, getting a firm beak hold of it, and then looks up at me with that look of trust…his little black beady eyes peering into mine. Then he cries out as he bounces out of my hand and swoops out over the low railing to the branches of the trees below me. My day is now filled with joy, even though my heart yearns for the miracle of a rainstorm to douse the fire enough so that the crews could get a handle on it and I wouldn't have to leave my beloved nest high above the Selway.

    I went back in the lookout amid all the boxes with my summer's worth of supplies on the floor, and opened the cabinet drawer on the west wall, one that I hadn't cleaned out as of yet. Old journal logbooks, writing paper, and underneath it all were all the anniversary cards that Judy and I had given each other at Indian Hill. I thumbed through them all, reading the sentimental greetings we shared living in paradise. After going through them, one for every one of the 22 years we spent together up here, I decided not to throw them into one of the boxes, and to leave them here instead, where they belong. I said a quick prayer that the lookout would still be standing once the fall rains came. With knowing that God was listening, I went back to watching over the Slims Fire to keep the fire crews informed of unseen fire activity.

🌲 *Journal notes for July 21st from official logbook...*

0530 hours...sky conditions clear, 65 degrees at the lookout, calm winds.

0550 hours...Lolo Hot Shots to Indian Hill   Heading down ridge to work line.

Indian Hill to Lolo Hot Shots   10-4, smokes showing up in draw below you. Can't tell if it crossed creek.

0552 hours...Wilkinson to Indian Hill   Fire behavior this A.M.?

Indian Hill to Wilkinson   Southeast and west sector most active this morning. Last night fire fairly active from 1630-2000. No torching after 2000.

Wilkinson to Indian Hill   Heavy helicopters arriving today for water show.

0655 hours...Activity picking up. Smoke lying across ridge where crews are working.

0712 hours...Indian Hill to Division Bravo   Good smoke coming out of draw ½ mile to the north of your line. Can't see anything significant coming out of Meadow Creek bottom, but trees block my view to the bottom of canyon.

0745 hours...Indian Hill to Division Bravo   Increase in fire activity upslope in the draw.

Division Bravo to Indian Hill   Fire activity happening along Meadow Creek right now.

1050 hours...Indian Hill to Kirkpatrick   Medium ship dropping water on your fire.

1128 hours...Indian Hill to Kirkpatrick   Lower smoke along

Meadow Creek starting to cook.

1223 hours...Indian Hill to Kirkpatrick Some spotting to the south of draw, mid slope. Smoke getting really thick at upper end of burn on west side. Can't tell the extent of the run.

1520 hours...Indian Hill to Kirkpatrick There's increased fire activity in the draw where helicopter was dropping earlier.

1750 hours...Air Attack plane over fire besides 2 helicopters.

I woke up on the morning of the 22nd, after another night of tossing and turning, keeping a vigil on what the fire was doing, praying like heck that it wouldn't breach Meadow Creek and race up to my exposed, densely tree-covered ridgetop while I was zonked out. I ate a quick breakfast of some oatmeal and cantaloupe, giving the rind a good toss over the railing for my ground squirrel pets fifty feet beneath my feet. As their *eyes in the sky,* I gave another update to the fire crew.

0745 hours...Indian Hill to Idaho Panhandle Fire Crew The west end of the fire was fairly active last night with a good-size smoke down in Meadow Creek.

1125 hours...The Incident Commander of the Type II Slims Fire Team, Stan Benes—my former lookout boss and friend—came up from the O'Hara Fire Camp for a visit to check out the fire and to see how I was doing. He did inform me that they had all the fire wrap down at camp that we'd need to protect the lookout.

After Stan got in his rig and started driving in his Forest Service green pickup down the road, he stopped at the top of the short uphill grade, at the spot where you get the first glimpse of the tower. He got out of his rig and took a picture of the tower, maybe thinking that it might be the last time he'd ever see it standing.

I continued my vigil, staring out at the fire from the west-side catwalk, noticing something that scared the hell out of me. Besides the choking smoke, there now was *something else* that concerned me. Out on the catwalk, besides the ash that I'd been seeing of late, were burned twigs and needles starting to cover the 2x6 planks! Then I got to thinking about the cedar-shingled roof that could easily catch fire from one of these firebrands. Convinced that the fire would jump Meadow Creek anytime now, I couldn't help but think that the fire wrap that Stan was talking about would be soon be used.

1340 hours...Lolo Hot Shots to Indian Hill   Can you see our mirror flash?

Indian Hill to Lolo Hot Shots   You're too deep in the canyon for me to see it apparently.

Lolo Hot Shots to Indian Hill   Spot down on Meadow Creek acting up.

1620 hours...Wilkinson to Indian Hill   "Hang in there!"

I was "hanging in there", but just barely. The fire intensity was increasing and my nerves were getting a bit frazzled, as I thought back to 1997 when I wrote *Tarzan the Mountain Man & The Pete King Fire of 1934* up at Indian Hill. I remembered oh so well Tarzan's description of having to run from the Otter Butte Lookout that he built by himself, racing ahead of the Pete King Fire's flames that were licking at his heals. I remember the description that he gave of almost his last moments on this Earth...

He took one last look out over the railing and saw the orange-brown cloud billowing up from low in the Selway below his home. He raced into the lookout and called a May Day over the radio..."To all stations! Otter Butte is going 10-7 to escape the fire!" He didn't wait for a response, taking off down the steps, zigzagging down the trail to the creekside refuge from the firestorm.

The sky darkened. He could hear the roar sounding like the hurricane that he'd heard the day before. But this time he knew it wasn't a false alarm. This was the real thing. No more emergency planning. No more practice drills. He got down on all fours, grabbed the bucket and poured water over himself. Then he quickly grabbed the Pulaski and improved on the fireline, cutting it wider...throwing needles outside the moat that would hopefully protect him. Louder. The light of the afternoon was quickly being replaced by the darkening skies...the cloud of death billowing over his spot on the mountain getting thicker. He couldn't see a thing beyond the canopy of trees that he hoped wouldn't produce a widow maker when the winds bore down on him. The eight gallons of water hanging from the tree, wetted down the ground that he'd cleared of brush earlier. The gallon canteen was partially emptied into his mouth. The roar intensified. It was getting hard to breath. The tree umbrellas above his head started swaying in the wind. He started to feel the heat.

    Down on all fours again, he set up operations in the small stream, the icy-mountain spring water numbing him, but giving him the only hope of seeing another day on the Earth. Louder. The freight train roar was almost more than he could stand. He bent over and stuck his head in the water as much as he could in the depression he'd already dug into the fold in the mountain. Then he raised up, the spray soaking more of his body. Louder. Darker. The heat intensified. He felt the water getting warmer. He sunk back into the tiny creek. It was the last thing he could think of doing before he was cremated or saved from the fire-breathing monster.

    He saw the reflection against the water, heard the hurricane roar and the crackling that told him that the Pete King Fire was testing his defenses. He could hear the cracking and crashing of the trees through the roar. He could hear his heart pounding. Heat beyond what he thought he could take. Flames. Choking-thick smoke. He didn't look up. He just *kept staying low, his mouth a half inch above the warming mountain stream, feeling like he was going to soon find out what it was like to die in a fiery death...*

    I began to think, where would my safety zone be if the fire made a run up towards the ridge? There was nowhere on my west side that could remotely be considered a safety zone. But maybe off to my east, down in Bluff Creek, I could be safe from a raging Slims Fire. Knowing the mountain like the back of my hand, I knew of a spot where I could hide out, which was surrounded by huge rocks. Sure, that's where I'd go to make my last stand. The only thing that I wouldn't have was a small creek like Tarzan had up off of Otter Butte. If I had to make a run for it, I'd at least take a couple of canteens with me.

    At 1800 hours I made a cell phone call to Judy, who was back in Wisconsin visiting her parents, to tell her what was happening. I gave her the update on the fire, and that I thought I'd probably be evacuating pretty soon. But more than anything, I just needed that *connection* with the woman who knew more than anybody else what I was going through on the mountaintop. I was chatting away, seemingly without a care in the world other than to connect with her 1800 miles away...but feeling like she was right here with me. "You need to stop chatting and get your things packed up in the truck and come down off that mountain!" she insisted.

    With the phone call cut shorter than I wanted, but realizing that she was right...I needed to start putting my evacuation plan into motion— even though the official word to abandon ship hadn't come across the airwaves yet. I ate a quick last supper of canned beef stew and washed it down with spring water. Then I began the slow process of hauling all of my boxes down the steep four flights of stairs and into the bed of my Nissan pickup. Up and down I went, load after load of my summer's worth of supplies ready for the trip down the mountain.

At 2000 hours I got a radio call from the Salmon River lookouts who apparently had been monitoring the Nez Perce channel, wishing me all the best. Then I got a call from Dutcher up on Pilot Knob wishing me the same. That was followed with a call from Tom up on Shissler Peak Lookout.

2130 hours...Wilkinson to Indian Hill   We want you to come down to the Slims Fire Camp for a short stay until the fire cools down.

2210 hours...Wilkinson to Indian Hill   Check in with security when you reach camp.

Everything was done except locking the door and catwalk gate, and leaving my beloved home. But it was hard to leave, not knowing if the tower would still be standing by the time I got the chance to fire wrap it. The good thing...I hadn't heard yet if the fire had jumped Meadow Creek. But the bad thing was that while living down at the Fenn Ranger Station bunkhouse, I wouldn't have a clue to what the fire was doing once it did cross the creek.

At 2225 I turned off the Coleman lantern and locked the door to my domain, then closed and locked the catwalk gate. Using my Forest Service headlamp I made my way again down the steep stairs and down the lookout path that led to the log cabin. I went over to the signpost and carried the Indian Hill routed sign inside the cabin, and locked the door. Dejected to end my lookout season so early, but oh-so-glad not to get swept up from a raging forest fire, I got in my pickup and started the ignition, saying a prayer that the wind wouldn't pick up and carry the flames up the mountain and seal off my only escape route. My 12-mile long driveway was entirely on the west side of the mountain where the fire would burn if it crossed over to the east side of Meadow Creek.

It was a nerve-wracking trip down the road, worried stiff

that the fire could make a run up the mountain and block my only escape route. My big concern was that I was getting *closer* to the fire, not distancing myself from it while I made my way through the Little and Squirrel Creek drainages west of the lookout. I continued to make my way west, then northwest, closing in on my goal of getting off this totally exposed roadway in the middle of the night. Once I crossed over onto the Selway River side of the divide with Meadow Creek, I finally breathed a huge sigh of relief, being away from the direct path of the fire.

I knew that I had been left on the lookout this long to be the "eyes" of the fire crews and I was glad to have done it.

Thankfully my prayers were answered as I got down my lookout road safely, and then down to the Slim's Fire Camp on the Selway, where I checked in to the Security folks who were anxiously waiting for my arrival.

So now I was safe, but the lookout was not, and could soon be a prime target for the flames that any day now could be sweeping up the mountain, unless we got some much-needed rain.

I waited patiently at camp for the word that I could go back with my work partner, Bo Lane, to fire wrap the tower. A couple days went by when I worked at the station, stayed at the bunkhouse, and ate the scrumptious meals down at the Slims Fire Camp.

Bo and I finally got the word from the Incident Commander, Stan Benes, that we had permission to wrap Indian Hill. One requirement, though, was that we could only do it with a Safety Officer up at the site, watching in case the fire threatened us, and to be there if one of us fell off the tower. I was happier than a clam to go back up to save my lookout from burning to the ground.

Bo and I, along with a crew from fire camp, arrived at the lookout on what proved to be a good day to begin wrapping the log cabin and tower, with the fire activity considerably slowing down. Meadow Creek had finally been breached, but the fire stayed safely well below the Indian Hill Road, allowing us access to the mountaintop. While the fire crew started working on the cabin, Bo and I took a couple rolls of the heavy, impossible to rip, giant-sized aluminum foil up to the boardwalk to cut to length with our utility knives. We began the process up at the top, with me using the hammer stapler, and fire wrap, to seal off the cedar-shingled roof, using a ladder that I had stashed up on the west side of the catwalk. Up and down the tower we went to cut the rolls of fire wrap, and staple them to the outriggers, and then to the shutters that we dropped down over the four banks of windows. We covered the catwalk, then started working on the railing, leaning over the edge to staple the "aluminum foil" to the 2x4's. With the fire crew making good progress on the log cabin, Bo and I were also making good progress on the lookout. Bo, an ex-Smokejumper, was more comfortable hanging from the tower while wrapping the legs, and cross braces, while I belayed him. With the Safety Officer watching like a hawk for any significant increase in fire activity, we kept making the 41-foot tower look like the Tin Man from the Wizard of Oz. Wrapping the tower *wasn't* a fast process, with Bo having to stop when he ran out of wrap, and going down to the boardwalk at the base of the tower to cut some more pieces. And with the fire weather cooperating, with the winds not fanning the flames below us, we were allowed to finish the project the following day.

On July 26th I finally could breathe easier, knowing that the tower and the 1929 log cabin were protected from what could be a raging Slims Fire any day now. I waved goodbye to my lookout summer home, shining brightly in the smoke-filtered sun.

My boss, Bill Wilkinson, sent Bo and I on a 10-day hitch to reroof the Lost Horse Cabin, that's located about 20 miles southwest of Hamilton at Lost Horse Pass on the Bitterroot Divide. It was while we were working up there that the Slims Fire *finally* made a dramatic run, with Bill Wilkinson capturing the blow-up on July 30th, from high above the lookout in a helicopter. When I got back to the house after working up at Lost Horse, I got the news of the run with a message on my machine that stated that the tower was—thank God—still standing! The other good news I got was that the fire folks were going to send me up to Coolwater Lookout for the rest of the fire season.

Staffing Coolwater, where my friends, Tom and Betsy, were lookouts, was such a different experience than being up on Indian Hill. For one, the tower was just a ten footer instead of 41 feet. The lookout was on an open ridge, ideal for ridgerunning. And the best part was the two alpine lakes that sat nestled beneath the tower. They sat like two huge swimming pools, tempting me to dive into their cool depths every day.

The only drawback to Coolwater, though, is the road...it is rougher than a corncob, with huge rocks that threatened to rip out your differential. But I luckily had a beefy 4WD to meet such a challenge, and did make it up to my adopted summer home.

Going to a lookout's spring is always special, and Coolwater's was no exception. Located along the road and a quarter mile hike by trail, I went to it almost daily for my water needs. There even was a ladle to use for drinking. Sorrel, that was already turning orangish red, and beargrass, adorned the slopes below Coolwater, made for a beautiful alpine scene. The Golden Mantled ground squirrels, like at Indian Hill, were my little pets on the mountaintop. I coaxed them with peanuts, getting them to climb up my legs to get the prize from my outstretched hands. And the pikas, the cute little rock rabbits, I could hear *eeeeking* in the surrounding scree slopes. I went swimming almost every day in Fire Lake, and every once in a while down in the lower Coolwater Lake. That lake had a gray snag from an old avalanche poking out of it about a hundred and fifty feet from shore. When I went down to the lake for a dip, I would swim out to the snag and touch it before returning to shore. Fire Lake, the warmer of the two lakes, and a shorter distance to hike, required negotiating a steep rocky ridge that spined off to the northeast of Coolwater. A favorite lake for moose, I oftentimes swam with the bulls, cows and even calves, hoping like heck that they wouldn't come after me.

There were two lookouts at Coolwater...the hip-roofed 10-foot tower with a cab the same size as Indian Hill, and the original, gable-roofed lookout built in 1929, which sat about a hundred feet to the southwest of the tower. It was nicknamed the "rat house" because it reeked of pack rat urine, which was obviously their hide-out. You only had to go in there for firewood, so you purposely made your visits to the old, rotting-away lookout short. Coolwater had a small lookout cookstove with an extremely small firebox and an oven which I used to bake cookies during my six-week stay up there. Not wanting to waste propane for the miniature-size stove, I cooked a lot of my meals on the wood cookstove.

Usually at Indian Hill I had projects to do for the summer to keep busy, and I found a much-needed project at Coolwater to work on—building a new "kitchen" table to replace the old ugly one. So I got the dimensions and made a quick trip back to Montana to cut the lumber for a brand new table for the lookout. I ended up ripping and cutting leftover beams and other boards I had from building our log-sided house on Lolo Creek.

Back at Coolwater, I kept up a vigil for any new fire starts, and chatted with the few visitors that made it up to the mountaintop. Everything about my time up on the lookout was pleasant, including all the hikes that I did from the firetower. One day off I ended up ridgerunning out to the east to the old Louse Point lookout site, which was complete with an ancient alidade that was planted in the rocks. Most mornings I would do my walkabouts that spoked out to the west and east to get views back to the lookout on the sharp rocky point. But the only troubling thing about my stay up on Coolwater was observing the last breaths out of the Slims Fire near Indian Hill. With the last major run happening while I was at Lost Horse, I now had glimpses of light tendrils of smoke still coming from the 12,000-acre fire. It was a little nerve-wracking to watch smokes just below my summer home. But I knew that they had fire crews monitoring it up there, and the tower still stood tall on that lonely ridge 16 miles away, shining bright with its fire wrap still attached to every piece of wood on the tower.

    The inside of Coolwater Lookout became a construction zone, with me screwing, gluing, doweling, and sanding the small table. I even made two drawers for utensils and pencils and pens. As a finishing touch I applied three coats of varnish, sealing it to any water spills.

    During my stay my keen lookout eyes caught a number of new lightning-caused forest fires, which I reported to Fenn Dispatch and kept monitoring afterwards. I had a really nice visit with my old friend, Ray Kresek, author of *Fire Lookouts of the Northwest,* spending an afternoon chatting about the Slims Fire, and feeding my little Golden-mantled ground squirrel pets peanuts. Like at Indian Hill, I watched the hawks, eagles, turkey vultures, and ravens play on the lookout winds. But I couldn't get the gray jays to be comfortable enough to eat out of my hand up here. I woke up to the most awesome sunrises coming up over the sawtooth crest of the Bitterroot Divide, and equally great sunsets out over Oregon. One special scene, besides the millions of acres that I looked out over, was staring at El Capitan in the Bitterroots, an impressive monolith standing at 9,999 feet high! And I got to watch the incredible star shows, and rainbows arching their backs in the surrounding mountains after a good rain.

My season on Coolwater came to abrupt halt on September 22nd with a Gulf of Alaska Low Pressure blanketing the ridge with eight inches of snow, finally snuffing out the last of the Slims and surrounding fires. And the best part...my summer home was still standing tall across the Selway!

On September 24th I finally got to go back to reunite with my "friend in the sky" at Indian Hill and say a proper goodbye for the season! My heart leaped with joy when I came around the last bend in the road and saw that indeed my home was still intact. The fire crews had already removed the fire wrap for the long winter ahead, so it no longer looked like the Tin Man.

I got out of my rig at the log cabin that was also unwrapped. All the fire crews had gone. I was all alone. It felt sad that other than the two weeks I'd spent on Indian Hill, my summer was cut short by the Slims Fire. But I definitely felt privileged to have been sent up to Coolwater to experience that lookout for a wonderful six weeks!

I wandered up the lookout path, with just a few bright yellow sulphurflowers still adorning the mountaintop. I'd have to wait another nine long months to see the beautiful phlox and beargrass adorn the ridge. Although the lookout was spared, the stately alpine firs and lodgepoles were not. Blackened trees were everywhere, even off into Bluff Creek, where the fire apparently eddied into that canyon. Looking just to the north of the ridge, where the outhouse once stood, only charred wood remained. I climbed the steep lookout stairway and unlocked the catwalk gate to again be on my summer home. Up on the catwalk I could see all the destruction caused by the Slims Fire...charred trees surrounding the tower and down into Meadow Creek and off to my east in Bluff Creek. I could see that all the trees on the ridge to the southwest of the tower that led to the large meadow that I often hiked to, were totally burned. But what somewhat surprised me were all the islands of green trees among the black. And best of all, I found out on the way up here, that the spring was still an untouched Eden.

It would take me a while to get used to my new view when I returned next summer to my nest above the Selway. But I knew that new trees would sprout to replace the thousands and thousands of trees that met their demise this summer. But most importantly was that my summer home did not burn to the ground like I feared it might. I still had Indian Hill to come back to, to once again sway with the westward breezes, to live through the thunderstorms that swept out of the southwest, to witness the beauty of the rainbows after the storms, and watch my elk and deer neighbors cautiously make their way through the clearing beneath my feet.

As I drove back down the lookout road, I stopped at the top of the first uphill grade leaving the mountaintop and got out of my rig like Stan Benes had done on July 22nd. There I took a picture in my mind, reminding me what I had to come back to next summer.

I gave a salute to the tower that stood so lonely without its inhabitant, got back in my pickup and drove away to come back another day!

The early stages of the Slims Fire

The Slims Fire getting more active

*July 22, 2003
The day I
evacuated
the lookout*

*Dramatic
picture of the
tiny tower
threatened
by the huge
fire on July
30, at 6:40
p.m.*

*The wrapped
lookout with
nearby flames*

The tower and log cabin threatened by the Slims Fire

Coolwater Lookout

Fire Lake where I swam everyday

Tom and Betsy at their summer home up on Coolwater

My hike from Coolwater to the old Louse Point alidade

Table that I built at Coolwater Lookout

Staffing Coolwater Lookout in 2003 checking out fire east of tower

Below: Feeding Golden Mantled ground squirrel peanuts at Coolwater

Above: Ray Kresek on a visit to the lookout

Author at the lookout

Sunset from Indian Hill Lookout

Sundance

🌲 August 24th, 2020 Day 3

1900 hours   Perched high above the elevated valley, at the head of a steep talus slope, where nobody probably ever set foot, 500 feet from my mountaintop home at Sundance Lookout, I watched and waited patiently for my favorite furry little critters, the pikas, to announce their presence. Like watching water boil, not a peep came from the large boulder field at my feet. Suddenly a flash before me, a hawk dive-bombed the area, twenty feet above the lichen-covered rocks, swooping up and landing in a nearby alpine fir tree. *Eeeeek…eeeek…eeeek!* The steep, rocky mountainside came alive with the warnings of one pika to another that there was danger nearby. *Eeeeek…eeeek.* More signals to watch out for what now was watching them from the perfectly shaped fir. I listened to the *eeeeks* until the hawk flew off and the pikas were out of danger. Then constant *eeeeking* slowly faded to the sound of the wind blowing through the arms of the Christmas tree-shaped fir trees. After hearing the pikas from my favorite place to hike to after hours, I slowly made my way back through the beargrass-covered clearing below my lookout to the 25-foot tower to watch another incredible sunset from up high.

Since retiring from Indian Hill in 2008, it's been ten years now since I became the volunteer "closer" up on Sundance Lookout in northern Idaho. It is Day 4 in my 40-plus-day stay on the mountaintop. I'm sitting good with 65 gallons of water in cubitainers out on the catwalk, three 5-gallon tanks of propane that last eighteen days apiece, and a six-week supply of food in the miniature-size refrigerator and in tubs outside. I've got plenty of fire report forms to call in forest fires and an oriented, and historic, Osborne Firefinder to locate them in the middle of the 12x12-foot, all-glass house.

A big difference between my two lookout summer homes is the wind. Compared to Indian Hill, which got some big winds in storms, Sundance gets big winds a lot more frequently. "Calm" days are when the wind is blowing under 20 mph. I remember one time when a half-filled 5-gallon cubitainer was blown off the catwalk. Another time a tote filled with can goods got blown around the deck like it was a leaf. My view of the Selkirk Crest is like my old view of the Crags. Instead of Big Fog Mountain, East Peak, Fenn Mountain and Chimney Peak, it's Hunt Peak, Gunsight Peak, Mount Roothaan and Chimney Rock. The high mountain peaks to the northeast of Sundance yearn for me to climb them, and check out the mountain lakes like I did in the Crags. Instead of looking down on the incredibly beautiful, deep Selway River valley at Indian Hill, I look out at the equally beautiful 19-mile long Priest Lake at my feet. I love watching the sailboats tack back and forth across the wide lake, reminding me of Dad's sailing days on Lake Michigan.

So, which lookout do I feel closer to? I must admit that I feel a deeper attachment to my old home on Indian Hill. The wonderful beginning to our lookout lives in 1974, with Judy and Fritz, will always be my favorite year on my favorite lookout. After 35 years on Indian Hill and ten years on Sundance, they definitely have both gotten into my soul. They are like two best friends that I miss when I'm not up on their mountaintops. Someday I'd like to return to Indian Hill to see my old friend in the sky. The two adventures I've had on my two mountaintop homes have changed me. Living on a fire lookout for 45 seasons will do that to a person.

Like at Indian Hill, my days up at Sundance are filled with keeping a constant vigil for forest fires. This late in the fire season they can still happen at any time, like in 1967 when a lightning-struck tree 400 feet from the lookout turned into a 55,000-acre firestorm on September 1st, that killed two firefighters, Lee Collins and Luther Rodarte. The origin of the fire is marked with a sign Ray Kresek and his son, Dave, and friends, Rod Fosbeck, Tom Weitz and Pam Aunan, put up memorializing the two men who gave their lives fighting the fire. (Because the old sign was damaged from heavy snows over the years, Jackson Conlin of the fire crew, routed a new sign in the summer of 2021, with plans on putting it up at Sundance in 2022). The memorial and the thousands of gnarly-gray weathered snags in the area, are a constant reminder not to let my guard down, making lookouts at least every twenty minutes throughout the day. Today, though, I am also watching my five pet blue grouse do a tour around the tower, jumping from rock to rock, pecking at the low vegetation. I'm also keeping my eyes on a Columbian ground squirrel that is devouring the muskmelon rind I threw off the catwalk railing earlier. And then there's the Golden Mantled ground squirrels and chipmunks to check out. It's a busy place up on Sundance today.

1705 hours My chipmunk alarm goes off below the tower, telling me that there's some large bird scoping out the ridge. Immediately I go out to see what the commotion is all about. Not a hawk or an eagle, but a raven flies by, catching the built-up afternoon winds.

1800 hours The tower is shaking as I go out to have a look and see three visitors climbing up the 46 steps to my small living quarters. Soon a dad and his two sons break through the catwalk opening for a visit to a real live lookout. I introduce myself, point out some landmarks, and ask if the kids would like to see how I located forest fires. Excitedly they file in after me, and I tell them that I live up here and am Smokey the Bear's helper. Then I explain to them how to use the Osborne Firefinder, letting the kids see through the peephole sight with them standing on the foot-high lightning stool. I tell them that if a lightning storm is around, I'd be standing on the stool with glass-insulated feet to keep from getting shocked from a direct lightning strike on the tower. I tell them about the wildlife that

I see and explain that I'll probably be up here until the first part of October. Thrilled to share my lookout experience with the kids and parent, fifteen minutes later they leave my all-glass house on stilts to their world below.

🐝 Day 5

1400 hours   My Forest radio comes alive with Engine 1151 announcing that they are responding to a report of a smoke up Hunt Creek. I am put on full-scale alert, with that drainage only six miles north of me. The two things that you never want as a lookout is for somebody else to report a smoke that you should have seen, or calling in a false smoke, something that looks suspiciously like a smoke but isn't, like a clearing in the mountainside, or a cloud of dust from a road, or a waterdog—patches of ground fog after a rain, and then having the fire crew chasing after a ghost. I scope out the Hunt Creek area, hoping that I wouldn't discover that I had missed a smoke. Ten minutes of searching and I breathed a huge sigh of relief that the fire wasn't showing up to one lone lookout up at Sundance. I breathed another sigh of relief when the fire crew reported that they got the human-caused fire contained and controlled at $1/10^{th}$ of an acre.

1700 hours   In need of a hike, and some huckleberries, I checked out to Couer d' Alene Dispatch, grabbed a pot off the three-burner stove, secured my bear spray to my belt in case I ran into a grizzly, locked the catwalk gate and climbed down the three flights of stairs to my path to the east of the tower. I made my way through the beargrass to the south of the pika perch, and carefully negotiated my way down a steep, rocky slope to my super-secret huckleberry patch. When I got there I couldn't believe my eyes! Instead of heavily laden with huckleberries, there was hardly a berry to be found. I ate what few I could pick, then decided to continue hiking along the open ridge to the prominent rocky knob a couple hundred yards to the east, to do what lookouts do the best... take in the incredible view. My summer home looked like a stick-model, the tower three-quarters of a mile away to the west, the Selkirks standing high and majestic off to my north, and Lost Creek and Soldier Creek drainages lying right at my feet. I gazed across the saddle before me, at the huge rock wall a quarter-mile away. Two-hundred yards long east to west and a hundred feet high, I've hiked up to it and around it before. Suddenly my visual tour was interrupted by a familiar screeching, coming from high above the rock wall. I arched my neck and cast my vision on a huge, majestic golden eagle soaring over the country. I watched it do a few circles, then it came in for a landing at the top of the rock buttress. Stretching out his wings, I could see the white patches in the golden feathers as he came in for a landing. Totally blown away, I watched the top of the bluffs, the eagle looking pretty big at even four-hundred yards. I stayed glued to my seat on the rocky knob and kept my eyes peeled at the dark eagle. Then I heard more screeching, as another golden eagle came flying over the rock wall, coming in for a landing right next to its mate. I sat there in amazement, seeing two golden eagles land on the rock fortress that I now called Eagle Mount. Wishing I had brought my camera and binoculars, I watched the eagles moving about until one took flight and holy cow, was flying straight for me! Closer and closer it got, as it approached the rocky knob. Closer. I didn't need to have binoculars for this one, as he flew right over my head! I watched it as it continued past me, and off to the south of the tower. Then I turned my attention back to eagle number one to see if it would join its partner. But it didn't move, settled onto the top of "Eagle Mount". Rating this one of the best experiences of my Sundance career, I hiked back to the lookout filled with the majesty of the mountain.

🌿 Day 6

0700 hours   A herd of six mule deer show up to the west of the tower. Two bucks and four does. I watch them as their leader takes them on a tour of the mountaintop.

1130 hours   Flying ants cover the north-side railing. A cedar waxwing and some little unidentified yellow birds take advantage of the moment and gorge themselves on the unsuspecting ants.

🌿 Day 7

0830 hours   I had a first this morning. Walking back up the outhouse path after a bathroom visit, I noticed a man and woman in jogging shorts just below the lookout tower. Without seeing a 4-wheeler, side-by-side, or pickup in the parking area, I asked how the heck they got there. "By running!" they exclaimed. "Took us 2 ½ hours."

I quickly did the math in my head. Ten miles and over 4,000 vertical feet in elevation gain, I was more than impressed. "You sure made it in good time," I said, noticing that they weren't even out of breath. We introduced ourselves, and soon Darren and Katie were off, running back down to where they came from, the two very in-shape people disappearing around the first bend in the steep and rugged primitive lookout road.

On *Day 8, August 29th*, there was a Red Flag Warning for high winds, and a very high fire danger as a result. I didn't get any fires, but I did get Ryan, a visitor, who used those high winds to his advantage, flying a large kite on the open, beargrass-covered ridgetop. I watched in amazement at the aerial acrobatics that the kite made, going high above the lookout one minute, then diving almost to the ground the next. Then a wind gust took the kite high above the tower again, doing swirls—going up and down, up and down, flying erratically. For over an hour Ryan gave one lookout above him a lot of pleasure, watching him fly his kite.

    Sundance Lookout is the northern terminus of the Tour of Idaho, a grueling, 2,000-mile trailbike trek that starts in the southeast corner of the state at the Utah border. Today was my lucky day. Stuart Schiff, the 76th biker to ever finish the adventurous, 10-day trip, arrived at the lookout, with his friend, Dylan Knight, and girlfriend, Kristiana, trailing behind in a pickup. I had met other bikers up at Sundance who had done the trail, but none that spent enough time here for me to learn much about the tour. They climbed the lookout steps to take a bunch of pictures, and to sign the guest log, and I asked a bunch of questions—probing their minds about their journey. I found out that Stuart and Dylan had started out together, but on Day 7 Dylan had hit his hand on a snag leaning out into the trail, and broke his finger. Using electrical tape, they taped it up, and rode another fifty miles for help. Unable to continue on, Dylan waited for Kristiana to drive from North Carolina—where they lived—to pick him up. Having to go it alone, Stuart finished the tour by himself. Asking more about the arduous trek, they told me that most of the journey was on single and double (ATV) track, graveled roads, and some pavement. I found out that they were on the trail for up to 16 to 18 hours each day. They had seen lots of elk, moose, deer and antelope. Curious to find out why they did it, they both said "for the adventure!" I definitely could relate. After loading up Stuart's trail bike in the back of the pickup next to Dylan's motorcycle, we said our goodbyes, from two adventurers to another.

🐝 Day 9

1500 hours The winds have cleared out all the haze from fires in Washington, Oregon, and California, making for crystal clear skies, and a great day to check out my far horizons. Snowshoe Peak, 60 miles off to my southeast in Montana in the Cabinet Range, stands tall at 8,700 feet. Clifty Mountain, far off to my east, at 6,700 feet lies just inside the Idaho border. Snowy Top, at 7,500 feet to my north, a quarter mile from Canada, is 35 miles away. A range of mountains beyond Snowy Top sits well inside Canada, a good 70 miles away. I glass over to the west, taking in Little Snowy Top at 6,800 feet on the U.S. side of the border. Then I long-eye more mountains in Canada that I have no clue to their names. I take out my binoculars and check out some more mountains to the west of Snowy Top. I focus in on an interesting knob with what appears to be a lookout tower on it. I bring out the maps to compare notes. Salmo Lookout appears to be too far east to be this lookout. I scan the map some more, finding Sullivan Lookout farther to the west. But it is too far west to be my mystery lookout. Then I take another close-up view, focusing in on what I now believe is a fire lookout north of the border. None of my maps show Canada, so I guess it will remain a mystery. I can see mountains far to my west, a good 80 miles away, which show up clear as a bell today. Off any of my maps they will also have to go without names.

Tour of Idaho riders 77 and 78 show up at the lookout parking area. Since they are too tired to climb the tower, I take the visitor log down and get their names, Kurt Anness and Jeff Stoess, on the official logbook. They told me that they ran into a huge thunderstorm that put down a lot of hail in southern Idaho, freezing them. They ran into bears, mountain lions, wolves, moose and elk. Their 200-plus mile grueling days, 60% on single track, simply wore them out. They said they definitely would never try it again. When asked what they liked about the trip, Kurt said the constantly changing terrain. They both echoed Stuart and Dylan's sentiments that they went for the adventure. We wished each other well, and I waved goodbye to two more adventurers as they motored away.

🐾 Day 10

0800 hours   Rain in the night has caused fog that covers the whole Selkirk Crest to my northeast. Snowy Top, Little Snowy Top, the mountains in Canada, including my mystery lookout, are also covered in low clouds. Tens of puffy white, attached-to-the-mountains clouds look suspiciously like smoke. But not to this 45-year trained lookout. I can hear Lost Creek, just off to my south, on this rare windless morning.

Fog is slowly creeping up on Sundance Mountain, a low cloud about to wrap the lookout in a thick gray blanket. It creeps closer, my view to the south and east down to a couple hundred feet. Just before my view is completely blocked, the fog starts to break up, creating openings, as I can again see the North and Middle Forks of the East River and all the way to Gisborne Lookout, my neighbor 10 miles away to the south. Eagle Mount to my east appears again as fog lifts and reveals the huge granite rock wall a mile away. I go out on the catwalk and deeply breathe in the refreshing rain-washed air. What a wonderful start to another great day on the mountaintop.

1130 hours   I'm entertained watching the cute little chipmunks scurry up the three-foot beargrass stalks, swaying back and forth, trying to get the seeds. I haven't seen the Columbian ground squirrels for about a week now. Remembering that they went into their burrows in late August up on Indian Hill, I figure that's what is going on here. And I haven't seen my Golden Mantled ground squirrel Rocky around of late. My furry little friend I know will be back, being too early for him to hide out for the next nine months.

🐝 Day 11

At last night's supper I finished eating the last of the green beans from the garden. I've also finished the garden tomatoes and fresh peaches. I will miss the garden produce and sweet, juicy peaches up here. But more than anything I miss Judy. It was a little tough leaving her this year. She had hip replacement surgery in early July. I became her helper for six weeks, helping her get dressed, putting on her compression socks, making the meals, doing the dishes, feeding the cat, watering the indoor plants and the garden, picking weeds, deadheading flowers, cutting the grass, and driving her to her doctor's appointments and physical therapy sessions. It was great to see her improvement over time, her ditching the walker, not needing the compression socks anymore, the pain decreasing, walking without a limp, negotiating the stairs in the house, and finally—after 6 weeks—being able to bend over, and drive again. When I waved goodbye to her at the house, leaving for Sundance, I felt confident she'd be able to handle everything by herself. So, as visitors ask me up here, "Do you get lonely?" I must admit that I do for Judy. The cell phone coverage is spotty on Sundance, but I do call her Sunday and Wednesday nights to hear how's she's doing. So far things with her are going good with her hip, except for a little pain once in a while. From high atop Sundance, I send her good vibes. I hope she feels them.

Today is September 1st, the 53rd anniversary of the big blow-up of the Sundance Fire when the raging inferno made a 25-mile run, burning 51,000 acres in just eight hours. Lee Collins and Luther Rodarte were in its path and didn't make it out alive. I'm extra alert today with the Very High fire danger rating. Every twenty minutes I do an extra careful scan of the endless mountains in every direction. After ten seasons up here, I know my country well, going over it again and again with the pile of maps I have in the lookout. Fire reports ready, Osborne Firefinder oriented, I'm ready in case I see a smoke appear in my seen area. After supper I know where I'm going—to the Sundance Fire Memorial site at the origin of the fire, to pay my respects to the two fallen firefighters.

🐝 Day 12

1350 hours   Winds from the north are making interesting wave patterns on Priest Lake, the leeward south sides of the large Kalispell and Baritoe Islands contrastingly smooth as silk. I can see a couple of motorboats struggling to make progress through the large waves.

1410 hours   A large unidentified hawk flies to the north of the lookout, heading east, doing a couple of circles around the big rock wall, then landing on Eagle Mount. Strangely I haven't seen the golden eagles since Day 5.

1430 hours   The afternoon forecast from Coeur d'Alene Dispatch calls for temperatures in the valleys to remain warm for the next four days, getting into the 90's. It's 75 degrees up here, the warmest it's been since I arrived. It's the first day I've been able to sit out on the catwalk in only a t-shirt. I'm loving this warmth up on Sundance.

🐝 Day 13

Living in an all-glass house, I can see forever. I revel in the fact that every day I can wake up to this spectacular view. It's what I live for, waiting for ten months of the year to return to the top of the world! With no blinds or curtains, the incredible view is what makes this 12x12-foot room seem much larger. I often lie awake at night looking out at the stars, light-years away, but very close to one lone lookout guy up on Sundance Mountain. Last night the bright full moon was beautiful. I went out on the catwalk and saw the shadow of the lookout cast on the ridgetop from the bright light. The mountains were all aglow. The open ridge to Eagle Mount was softly lit, inviting me to go on a moonlit stroll. But my fear of running into a grizzly quickly squelched any nighttime-hike ideas. Throughout the night I kept a vigil, constantly waking up, keeping track of the moon's progress across the night sky.

🌲 Day 14

I still have seen no sign of my Golden Mantled ground squirrel buddies for a while now. Apparently they have joined the Columbian ground squirrels in their underground burrows. And I haven't seen the grouse lately. Luckily I still do see an occasional chipmunk climbing the beargrass stalks. I miss the residents of the mountaintop like best friends.

But there is plenty of bird activity this morning. A bunch of olive-green yellowish unidentified birds are landing on the guy wires, on the railings, in the alpine fir trees, and on the ground around the tower. I can see flying ants swarming around the tops of the trees and some on my north railing, the reason for all the birds showing up this morning is to get an easy meal.

1320 hours   Hooray! My grouse buddies are back, making their way underneath the lookout on the exposed bedrock. I count three, down from the five I saw earlier. I follow them as they jump off the huge rock and make their way to the north of the tower, until they disappear from sight.

1640 hours   I get a real treat. Rocky, my Golden Mantled ground squirrel buddy finally shows up, scampering amongst the rocks on the southeast side of the lookout. Chipmunks, grouse, Rocky seen today. My life on Sundance is back to normal.

The temperature on the mountaintop is 82 degrees, the

warmest I've ever had it on lookout, here or up on Indian Hill in 45 years!

🐝 Day 15

Thanks to Chuck Petty, the previous volunteer lookout, I had huckleberry pancakes for breakfast this morning. Much to my surprise, when I arrived here I found a quart of huckleberries inside the coffee pot. Huckleberry pancakes, a three-state and Canada view, there's no better way to wake up.

1615 hours   I hear it before I see it, screeching high above the lookout to the south of the tower. I scan the skies and finally see my majestic golden eagle neighbor soaring a couple thousand feet above the ridge. I watch it fly off to the east, over Eagle Mount, before losing sight of him. It makes my day to again witness its majesty.

🐝 Day 16

When a Labor Day weekend visitor asked me yesterday the date so she could put it in the guest book, I suddenly realized it was September 5th, the exact day last year of my final chemotherapy treatment to cure my Lymphoma Cancer! When I told the visitors that I was now in remission we did a little celebration dance out on the catwalk.

It had been a long, tough year. No hiking, no biking, no kayaking, no swimming, no Black Hills Mickelson Trail bike trip with my adventure buddy, Gary Winek, no going up to Sundance last year. Judy was my main support, being my nurse for seven long months. I also had a lot of support from my brother and sister, my Bible Study group, and my many friends. Pam Aunan, my good friend and lookout coordinator for Sundance, sent me so much encouragement through cards, emails, and phone calls. And she offered the carrot at the end of the stick, the ultimate reward for beating cancer, she was saving my closer role up at Sundance for 2020. I never looked forward to anything so much and now I'm celebrating being back up on the mountaintop.

0920 hours   I do an inventory of my supplies. Day 16 on an 18-day propane tank. I should be switching to tank #2 soon. I'm down to 50 gallons of water out on the deck, which equates to using about a gallon a day. I definitely have enough to get to October. I have enough meat for 23 more meals. Then I have tuna and macaroni and cheese for four more meals. I brought along some freeze-dried backpack meals, just in case I run out of food. My munchies were running low until a very nice bear-hunter family gave me a bunch more to replenish my dwindling supply. Cheetos, my favorite, Cheez-its, Sweet and Salty trail mix, and crackers I now have safely stashed away in my tub out on the deck, ready to break into when I get one of my cravings for a snack.

1345 hours   The winds are picking up, making an eerie howling sound through my partially-opened west window. I can also hear it out on the catwalk, the loud, eerie whistling sound as it blows around some loose flashing on the roof. Forecasts call for strong winds tomorrow. Time to batten down the hatches.

1440 hours   The Forest radio comes alive with Gisborne Lookout calling in a smoke northeast of Jasper Mountain at 269 degrees in Section 28, Township 58N and Range 4W. Immediately I get out the binoculars to see if I can spot it too. I zero in on that location and yes...I can pick I up! Quickly I go inside and line the firefinder up on the smoke ten miles to my southwest. Grabbing the microphone, I report to Coeur d'Alene Dispatch that I'm getting 206 degrees to the fire. After clearing myself from the radio I ponder if I should have seen it earlier. Perhaps. But it wasn't putting up much smoke and Gisborne is half the distance to the fire than I am. I just feel good that Carol Taylor, my friend at Gisborne, found her first fire of the season. By 1608 hours, Engine 1161 reports that the East Side Fire was two tenths of an acre and the cause was unknown.

🐝 Day 17

    0800 hours   70 mph north winds rock the lookout. A chair out on the catwalk has blown against the railing. I take my totes inside to keep them from blowing away. I can feel the strength of the wind in the shaking of the tower. I can feel it in how wobbly I am when I stand. I can feel it with the shaking handwriting in this journal. A rainbow arches over Soldier Creek, the purple, aqua, yellow, and orange's tranquil beauty such a contrast to these hurricane-force winds. Wind-blown rain streaks the windows.

    0830 hours   The winds are so strong now that I guessed that they are maybe 100 mph! The rain turns to snow, the ground starting to turn white. The east-side railing, normally rock solid, is shaking like a leaf. The fire extinguisher, hanging by the door, is rocking back and forth, just like the tower. I pray that it doesn't fall over with me in it!

    0855 hours   A report comes over the emergency channel of an overturned canoe on Priest Lake by Papoose Island. Two rescuers are dispatched from a boat launch in Kalispell Bay to save the canoers. I've got my fingers crossed that they get to them soon.

    0902 hours   The rescuers report that they have eyes on three people on Papoose Island.

    0907 hours   All three people on board, safe and sound. I breathe a huge sigh of relief.

    1015 hours   A report comes through of a large tree that fell on a house. Another report of trees coming down in a campground. No injuries reported so far.

1030 hours   The East-Side Fire is showing smoke again from Sundance. The Priest Lake Fire crew is on it, reporting that it looks good and they will be mopping it up.

1040 hours   Extremely high winds still rock Sundance Lookout. I feel like a drunken sailor walking in the lookout with the tower shaking so much. I keep a constant lookout now for any new fire starts on this Red Flag day. Anything starting will really take off in this wind.

1135 hours   I spot a smoke far off on my southwest horizon. Excited to find a fire, I quickly line the Osborne Firefinder on my smoke. I get a 199 degree azimuth from Sundance. I grab my binoculars and zero in on the light-blue smoke. But where was it coming from? Just behind Hoodoo Mountain or further out on the Mount Spokane ridge! Calling Gisborne for a cross azimuth, Carol said she couldn't see anything. So I was on my own here. The smoke lies back down, hiding from my prying eyes from more than thirty miles away.

1145 hours   Another puff of smoke appears in the distance, triggering me into action. I immediately key the mike and call Dispatch to alert them of the smoke. I give them my azimuth and say it looks to be just past Hoodoo Mountain, my best guess. After I cleared myself from the radio, I yelled out, "Thank you, God!" I was so happy to have turned in a fire.

1148 hours   Indian Mountain calls in a cross azimuth of 180 degrees to Coeur d'Alene Dispatch. I quick run out Pam's azimuth and find my smoke is by the town of Blanchard, 38 miles away, well past Hoodoo Mountain.

1150 hours   Gisborne calls in a cross of 206 degrees, confirming the Blanchard location.

1500 hours   The Blanchard Fire shows a large brownish-colored smoke column, showing that it is making a run. My guess is that it's at least a couple hundred acres by now.

🐝 Day 18

0500 hours   I woke to the strangest sound on Sundance… complete silence. Not a stitch of wind anymore. But it was cold. 36 degrees this morning.

I got up and made a bacon-and-egg breakfast, then with a cup of hot chocolate in hand I went on a walkabout in the lookout yard, ending up at my pika perch to see if my neighbors were also up and about. It wasn't long and I heard an *eeeek* coming from high up in the steep talus slope. Then another *eeeek* from the same pika. Suddenly he appeared, my little furry companion scurrying over the boulders at my feet. I take sips of hot chocolate and wait for more pikas to announce their presence. Five, ten minutes I wait patiently— then without a peep another pika goes scurrying from boulder to boulder about a hundred feet below me. Then another one hops his way across the rocks without a sound. Filled with the enjoyment of watching them, I make my way back to the tower, now ready to start my official work day.

1100 hours   For some reason, strange looking large circles are etched into Priest Lake this morning. Not a boat can be seen.

No wind, no people. It's a welcome change up here on the mountaintop. Labor Day Weekend brought the crowds. 4-wheelers, side-by-sides, trail bikes, jeeps, pickups, and SUV's, they came one after another. Saturday's count was 67. Sunday's was a record with 120 people coming up to check the place out. Thankfully there is a sign at the bottom of the tower, announcing—**No Visitors, 2020. Please respect the health and space of the lookout.** The sign, because of the COVID-19 pandemic, keeps my lookout visitors down, but still tens of people made their way up here. They come for the incredible view, they come to see a real live Forest Ranger working on a fire lookout. Now I'm back to being all alone, just the way I like it, to soak up the wonderful lookout life by myself—at peace with nature.

1300 hours   Very little activity is seen of the fire I reported yesterday, which is good news.

1345 hours   I spot a fairly large smoke to my east at 50 degrees, 30 minutes, past the Jeru Peak Ridge, and call it into Dispatch.

1350 hours   Dispatch calls me back and said it was a 200-acre field burn. And the best part was he announces "Good eyes up there!" over the whole Forest radio network. His pat on the back from the fire organization really makes my day.

🐾 Day 19

On my walkabout this morning, with an insulated cup of tea in hand, instead of heading east to the pika perch, I go south to the top of another perch, a fifty-foot high bluff that overlooks Lost Creek. A couple *eeeeks* from pikas greet me from the scree slope below. I take a seat on a flat rock to absorb the morning. I sit there and wait, listening for some more pikas. Some birds fly by, one landing on a rock nearby. Fifteen seconds later the olive-green-breasted bird takes flight. Suddenly I catch *movement* out of the corner of my eye, very close by, in the rocks. I wait patiently for whatever it was to reappear. Then it sneaks out behind a slab rock about two feet away, a Golden Mantled Rocky appearing. He stands on his hind legs, staring straight at me, trying to figure out what the heck I was, his nose twitching a mile a minute. I remain as still as a statue, not wanting to chase him off. For a minute my little furry mountaintop buddy stays standing, nose constantly twitching. Maybe it was a slight movement I made, but then he scampers away, hopping down off the rock, and disappears from sight.

Thrilled with the moment, I hike back to the lookout for my morning check-in to Coeur d'Alene Dispatch. Back on the tower I got the second treat of the day when a small hawk lands on the east-side roof eave. All I see is his colorful feathers and talons, with him facing away from me. Trying to get a better look, the hawk takes flight and flies off to land in the top of a nearby snag. I watch him for a little while until he jumps off his perch and flies away. I'm on cloud 9 starting the day with these wonderful nature displays at Sundance.

1045 hours   I get another real treat this morning when I hear a screech coming from down in Lost Creek. I look out and find my golden eagle neighbor low in the valley beneath my feet, doing circles to gain elevation. I quickly go in the lookout, grab my binoculars and zoom in on the huge, 7-foot wingspan bird of prey. I can make out a white band at the base of its fan tail, and the familiar two white splotches on his wings. I can clearly see his head and even his probing eyes. Circle after circle he finally gets to the elevation of the tower. I let the binoculars dangle around my neck and I watch him get higher and higher until I lose him in the sun. I wonder to myself how can this day get any better?

🌲 Day 20

This morning's walkabout takes me to a place I'd never been before, a rock outcrop overlook a couple hundred yards to the southwest of Sundance. With my cup of tea in hand I make my way through the 1967 Sundance Fire graveyard of old gnarly-weathered gray Whitebark snags. At the overlook it was a picture-perfect scene with the tens of snags and the lookout in the distance. Off to my south, a couple dozen unidentified birds are flying erratically, up and down, and around and around, reminding me of the swallows up at

Indian Hill divebombing the lookout. I stay entranced by the aerial acrobatics, watching them fly over and between the large snags. I watch the Blue Angels of birds until I feel I should get back to the tower for a check for smokes. A great start to another fantastic day on the mountaintop.

1135 hours   The unidentified, dark-gray-and-white birds that I saw earlier are now divebombing the lookout, getting close enough I can almost touch them. Around and around they go above the tower, doing strafing runs of my home in the sky. Five minutes later they are mysteriously gone, disappearing from sight to one very entertained lookout guy.

1600 hours   I hear a creak and a loud crack, then louder. I peer down the ridge and see a large snag crash to the ground where I had walked only eight hours earlier. Amazing...it took fifty-three years for that snag to weaken enough to fall. And I was just hours from being smashed like a bug! I breathe a huge sigh of relief that I didn't end up being killed on my morning stroll.

🌲 Day 21

Huge fires rage across the west. California has lost over three million acres to wildfire. In Oregon, 10% of the population has been evacuated due to wildfire. In Washington, over 300,000 acres burned on Labor Day. And the fire I called in has grown to over 600 acres, near the town of Blanchard. All this has created a lot of smoke, and I am in the thick of it. My visibility is down to about eight miles. I'm praying for some rain to wash all this smoke away.

0942 hours   Little Blue Angel pilots strafe the lookout again, the still unidentified dark gray-white birds coming close to splatting into the railing. I watch their aerial acrobatics for a while before they fly off elsewhere.

1007 hours   Out on the catwalk I hear a plane rev up, far down below me, signaling to look down at the backcountry airstrip next to the Ranger Station to the northwest. Then I see it, a Cessna taking off and flying over Cavanaugh Bay. One year a Cessna's take-off nearly ended up in tragedy, when the pilot piled up into a bunch of trees. Thankfully the pilot and passengers walked away from the crash with no serious injuries.

The smoke is getting a little less thick. My visibility has increased to at least twelve miles. Hopefully no fires will start up beyond that distance.

1230 hours   Carol, on Gisborne Lookout is back on her tower. It feels good to have more eyes in the sky looking out for fires in these dry conditions.

🐾 Day 22

I wake to smoke so thick you could cut it with a knife. Visibility is now down to a half mile. I hope that no fires start today with no probing lookout eyes to spot them.

1430 hours   Screeching out over Lost Creek puts me on full-scale alert again to see my golden eagle neighbors. I glance out over the canyon to my south and instantly catch sight of an eagle circling below the ridge. I follow it until I see a second, and then amazingly I see a third eagle flying just twenty feet above the mountain to the northeast of the tower. Then one of them lands in snag. Quickly I go inside and grab my binoculars. But as soon as I get back to the catwalk it jumps off the snag and joins the other two in flight. I follow them until they disappear from sight. I stand there, excited to know I have not just two, but three golden eagle neighbors close by.

🐝 Day 24

Thick smoke still covers the ridge. I can barely see Eagle Mount, a mile away. Thick smoke also covers the whole Northwest. Spokane, Portland and Seattle have hazardous air quality. Schools are closed. People are being advised to stay indoors. I'm also staying inside, reading magazines, waiting patiently for the air to clear so I can go back to being a lookout again, scanning the hundreds of thousands of acres of forest around me for fires.

🐝 Day 25

I wake to an unusual sight for the last four days. I can finally see some nearby peaks over the smoky haze. Mount Roothaan, Gunsight Mountain, Hunt Peak, Jeru Peak and Mount Casey are showing up for me this morning. Missing from view, though, is Priest Lake, which I miss like a best friend. The weather forecast is for the smoke to clear in about four days. I can hardly wait to see to my far horizons again.

1700 hours   After checking out with Couer d' Alene Dispatch I put my plan into action of doing something a little different than going on a hike. I have the novel idea of just laying out in a soft bed of beargrass for a while. With my portable Forest radio and phone in hand I climb down the 46 steps and wander over to what looks to be the perfect resting spot just southeast of the tower. I nestle in the beargrass and lie back, my head propped up by a clump of the spindly, but soft vegetation that old timers used for bedding, which they called ticks. The late-afternoon, smoke-diffused Indian Summer sun warms me, almost putting me to sleep. Tiny ants crawl on my hands, flies buzz by my head, a grasshopper whizzes nearby, a soft breeze caressing me on this glorious afternoon resting spot below Sundance Lookout that looms over my head. After about an hour, I saunter back to the lookout, observing a burrow dug into the mountainside. It must be where my Columbian ground squirrel buddies hang out for nine long months. I miss the biggest of the ground squirrels, sad to know I wouldn't see them again until next season. "Have a good nap!" I say, then make my way back to my heavenly perch.

🐝 Day 26

0800 hours   Hooray! I can finally just make out Cavanaugh Bay on Priest Lake, at 4 ½ miles. Welcome back old friend!

Yesterday I got a real pat on the back from Chuck Petty, the lookout who left the huckleberries for me. He said that he and his Dad read *Tarzan the Mountain Man*, a book I just had published, and thought it was great! Soaking up the praise that Chuck had for my book, his comments made me feel really good.

1035 hours   The radio comes alive with the report of a 3 to 5-acre fire up the West Branch of the Priest River. That is normally in my seen area, but not today in this thick smoke. I only have about five mile visibility, and the fire's twelve miles away. The fire boss's request for a Type III helicopter is denied because of all the smoke.

1055 hours   Thousands of flying ants are back, covering my west and north-side windows and railings. I need a good wind to blow all these creeping, crawling flying ants away.

1130 hours   Some of the flying ants drift onto the south side of the lookout where I was sitting. Time to take refuge inside my glass house for a while, reading *One Man's Wilderness*, a book about Richard Proenneke's life building a log cabin on Twin Lakes up in Alaska, and his experiences with nature where no roads existed. Sometimes I felt like Richard, living all alone on a mountaintop in extreme northern Idaho, experiencing nature and journaling about it. Yes, I liked the sound of that...my Sundance Lookout like living in a remote cabin in Alaska. Although I have a road up here, I choose not to drive down it, my truck keys left dangling from the firefinder cabinet, unused for the whole six to seven weeks that I'm up here.

1215 hours   Joyful news! My grouse are back on the east side of the tower, scampering, then stopping, scampering and stopping to peck at the vegetation, doing a tour of my lookout yard.

Richard Proenneke's Journal for July 14th—"In the afternoon I popped some corn."

John Crawford's journal notes for September 16th—"Like Richard, I also popped some corn for an afternoon snack."

1423 hours   Report from West Branch Incident Commander is that the fire is actively burning and is up to 20 acres now. From Sundance it is still an invisible smoke due to all the smoke.

1552 hours   I hear cooing coming from the west side of the tower and look down to see five grouse, their gray-brown plumage blending into the twenty-foot rock outcrop at my feet. I watch them moseying along on the huge rock buttress, the plump grouse keeping me company.

Trouble down in the outhouse, 150-feet away at the edge of the woods to the north of the tower. A pack rat (bushy-tailed woodrat) has been chewing up my toilet paper the last couple days. How it squeezes into the outhouse is beyond me. And how it reaches up three feet to get to the toilet paper is even more baffling. My solution...take toilet paper down there every time I use it. One year I had a pack rat sneak inside the lookout at dusk. Yelling and stomping my feet I luckily herded the rat back out and to where he came from. I had nightmares imagining trying to get some sleep with a noisy bushy-tailed woodrat leaving his calling card all over the lookout.

1640 hours   More cooing below the lookout. I gaze down at the ground and count seven grouse now, scurrying around and pecking at the vegetation. I stand there in amazement knowing that I have that many grouse neighbors on the mountaintop.

1800 hours   I've never seen this before. Usually the flying ants fly away after a while. But tonight they stayed, thousands of them covering the east and south side railings and catwalk. Oh, how I wish we'd get a good wind—that Sundance is famous for—to send them all away!

🐝 Day 27

0700 hours   The flying ants left during the night, leaving a few stragglers behind, as I discovered ants in my tea cup, coffee pot, on the floor, on the chairs, and on the counter and table. I'm hoping that was the last I'll see of them this year.

0800 hours   My walkabout takes me back to the pika perch for a little pick me up after the sixth straight day of extremely smoky skies. I sit my butt down on a comfortable rock and watch and listen. Five minutes into my vigil, with no sign of the rock rabbits, I do a pika imitation to get one to answer. Nothing. Not a single reply. Then another five minute wait, and I finally hear an *eeeek*. Then more silence. After about twenty minutes, I hear another pika, then another one. Encouraged, I let out another imitation from my pika perch to join in the chorus. But no more response. Between sips of hot chocolate I wait patiently to hear, and hopefully see my little furry friends. Just before I get up to leave, I hear a pika coming from about thirty feet away! Then another loud *eeeek*, and better yet, movement beneath my feet. I focus in on the cute little rock rabbit scurrying over and around the boulders. I listen some more for the talus-slope resident who disappeared between the rocks, but don't hear anything. Filled with incredible joy now, I wander back through the beargrass to my little house on stilts.

1045 hours   As usual I hear the screech before I get a visual of my golden eagle neighbor. Searching out over Lost Creek I soon can see it, the huge 7-foot wingspan of the bird of prey. I follow it in flight until it lands in the top of a snag about a half mile to the southwest of the lookout. Quickly I go inside and get the binoculars and go back out on the catwalk and zero in on the eagle. I stayed glued to the binoculars, staring at it, and suddenly another golden eagle comes into view, flying just above the first one. I follow it in flight, soaring out over Lost Creek. Then I focus again on the eagle still perched in the snag. Suddenly it spreads its wings and takes flight, landing in another snag about 200 feet away. As I stare at it with binoculars, it doesn't stay there long and starts flying back towards the lookout. I trade the binoculars for my camera and zoom in on the eagle, snapping off a couple of pictures. Then it continues flying east, disappearing from sight.

1130 hours   I get another present. Hearing some cooing while I was reading *One Man's Wilderness* out on the catwalk, I peer over the edge and see three grouse on the huge rock outcrop to the west of the tower. I also see two chipmunks playing in amongst the grouse, which warms my heart, because I hadn't seen them of late. What a morning... pikas, golden eagles, grouse, and chipmunks. Despite the thick smoke, it's been a great day up on Sundance. Another good thing about today, a nice breeze is blowing out of the southwest, grounding all the flying ants.

All this smoke has considerably cut down the visitor traffic, to practically none at all. I'm enjoying this peace and quiet, being totally alone for days on end.

🐝 Day 28

1600 hours   Major discovery on the mountaintop. After missing seeing any Mountain Bluebirds here for the last few years, I finally saw one land in the top of a ten-foot alpine fir tree to the east of the tower. I stared at the fir, hoping to find out I wasn't just seeing things. Then a couple minutes later I saw the sky-blue Bluebird fly off to prove at least one was back where they used to have their summer home.

🐝 Day 29

0700 hours   A thick gray blanket of fog covers the ridgetop so I can't even see the ground! I take a sponge bath on this cold morning out on the east-side catwalk and freeze my little butt off. *Brrrrrr!*

🐝 Day 30

1500 hours   After nine long days of smoke and then fog, I can finally see out. I can see all 19 miles of Priest Lake. I can see Jeru Peak, Gisborne Lookout, Atlasta Mountain, Mount Casey, Schweitzer Ski Area, Lost Peak, South Baldy Lookout and North Baldy, Indian Mountain Lookout, Lost Creek, and Soldier Creek. Missing though is the Selkirk Crest, still locked in the clouds. And I can finally see the West Branch Fire, started many days ago. It's like my eyes have finally opened after more than a week. I'm finally back in business of being a lookout, which makes my day.

1930 hours   I called Judy and got some very sad news. My publisher, Dale Burk, had died. I was devastated. More than just a publisher of my two books, he became a good friend. After going over edits of *Tarzan the Mountain Man*, we would talk about our lives. Dale shared in his family's roots in Trego, a logging town in Northwestern Montana, where his Dad was a logger. I learned about his hunting trips, his fishing trips, and about the books he was working on. He will be dearly missed by me and many others. In the phone conversation with Judy I also found out that she was doing well, that the garden was about done for the year, about ordering firewood for the winter, about our cat, Zoey, climbing trees after squirrels and figuring out how to get down, and the Green Bay Packers victory over Detroit. The more we talked, the more I got to missing my partner, 250 miles and a seven-hour trip away.

🐝 Day 31

I got a phone call from my good friend, Kris Anderson, who just came down from Coolwater Lookout after a month-long stint. I found out that she saw a wolf up there. She also told me about her hikes to Fire and Coolwater Lakes. She said she really enjoyed reading my book. Her call really made my day.

1400 hours   Four hikers laced up their hiking boots at the lookout and took off on a hike to the prominent bare knob three miles to the east, a place I've always wanted to get to.

1800 hours   The ridgerunners are back, filled with stories of running into tons of huckleberries, grizzly bear scat, the report of a pond behind the ridge, and of a wonderful hike, lighting my interest to get out there some day.

🐝 Day 32

1115 hours   Honking off to my east gets my attention. I go to the east-side catwalk and gaze up at the sky, trying to locate the geese. But I didn't see anything. Then I finally see the flock of Canada Geese flying in the familiar V formation. But instead of flying south, they are flying east to west.

🐝 Day 36

Two days straight of rain and being totally fogged in has led to this...a crystal clear view to all my distant horizons sixty, seventy, even eighty miles away. Gone is all the smoke haze that blurred my view. The Canadian Rockies show up like they are right next door. The 1.13" of rain that I got for the most part has quieted the fire season (I can't even see the West Branch Fire today). Any more rain—or snow—will definitely put an end to it.

I ran out of salt a couple days ago. It's amazing how much I miss it when I don't have it anymore. Lately I've been having the cravings for snacks. Gone are my peanuts, granola bars, Snicker bars, and nearly out of popcorn. And I'm missing a nice big tossed salad, some fresh fruit (been out for weeks), tomatoes, green beans, zucchini, anything from the garden. Thoughts of having a 5-dollar fill-up at KFC, a Big Mac at McDonalds, and a chili and Frostee at Wendy's enters my mind.

Maybe I'm getting lonely is the reason I called my sister, my brother, my friend Gary, my lookout neighbor Carol Taylor, my friend Ray Kresek, and of course, Judy. I was celebrating being out of the fog, having a great view, and just to connect with those close to me. It definitely satisfied my case of the lonelies.

1730 hours A snow squall hits the ridgetop, frosting Sundance and the Selkirk Crest white. After the storm passes, I can see fog waterfalling off the Jeru Peak ridge—cascading into the head of Soldier Creek, a very rare sight.

🌲 Day 37

I wake to brilliant sunshine bouncing off the snowy ridges. Priest Lake lies hidden, beneath a layer of fog. Surrounding mountains look like islands in a huge sea of low clouds.

0855 hours I had a first in all the years I've been on Sundance. I heard an elk bugle, sounding like it was coming from over on Camel's Prairie, a few air miles to my north.

1048 hours Rarely have I ever seen the air so clear up here. The snowy-white Rocky Mountains in Canada, well beyond the border, stand out like they are right next door. The mystery lookout in Canada seems a lot closer than usual, but I know it's at least 50 miles away. It's a day to celebrate being alive to soak up all this beauty. I told my Bible study group before coming up here, that I feel very close to God up on Sundance, and today I definitely feel it.

1230 hours Two visitors, Frank and Tyler, spot my golden eagle neighbors before I do, as we watch two eagles flying over Lost Creek and land in a couple of snags a half mile southwest of the tower. It was as much of a treat for them as it was for me to spot the majestic birds of prey again.

1840 hours I watched a beautiful, golden, orange, pink-lit cloud sunset out over Washington, the best since I arrived in August.

🐾 Day 38

0845 hours   On a walkabout I ran into my blue grouse pets just west of the tower. It was good to see them after a long absence. I watched the four of them scurry around the beargrass. Then one started coming towards me, unafraid. It stopped about fifteen feet from me. I started inching closer to the large gray-brown-feathered bird, slowly erasing the distance between us. Closer. Stopping almost close enough to pet it, I froze, listening to him clucking away, getting a little too close for his comfort. Then he had enough and went off to join the rest of his clan.

1035 hours   More excitement on the mountaintop! My friend, Pam Aunan, called on the cell phone and said that she was in a Cessna with pilot Chuck Petty, flying straight at me! I stayed on the line and said I could hear them, but couldn't see them yet. Then, suddenly I picked them up, and yes...they were headed right for Sundance! I stood out on the catwalk, waving at my two friends who circled a couple hundred feet above the lookout. It was so much fun talking to Chuck and Pam on their aerial tour. Then Chuck—a Southwest Airline's pilot—flew out to the bare knob three miles to the east of the tower, where he wanted to backpack to this fall. With my cell phone in my ear and my hand waving at Pam and Chuck, they flew off to my northeast to take a tour of the Selkirk Crest on this fabulously beautiful clear fall day, where I finally lost contact with the two airborne adventurers.

🐾 Day 39

The warm Indian Summer weather has replaced the very cold temperature of the last couple weeks. Gone is the long underwear, gone is the wool sweater, gone is the parka, the wool hat and winter gloves, gone is the insulated jacket I wear inside my winter sleeping bag. The forecast calls for this nice weather to hold through this weekend. Maybe, I hope, it will last till my last day on the lookout a week from now.

0945 My lucky day! When I mentioned to John and Donna Beaulieu, a couple visitors, that I was running out of supplies, they graciously rewarded me with all kinds of snacks to satisfy my need for the munchies. A bag of White Cheddar popcorn, cashews and peanuts (my favorite), Gummy Bears, bubble gum, Sweet and Salty nut bars, and some chocolate chip cookies—to replenish my non-existent supply. I felt like I just won the million dollar lottery, I was so happy! I'll remember their visit while eating all the snacks they so graciously gave a hungry-for-snacks lookout. Thanks John and Donna.

The fire season is barely holding on. The West Branch Fire shows no more smoke from here, and I haven't heard a fire crew working it anymore. I haven't heard a peep from the Benard Fire either. With the fire danger only at Moderate now I can finally relax, doing lookouts every half hour now instead of every twenty minutes. I still have plenty of books yet to read. I've read twenty books and twenty magazines already. And I'm keeping busy writing the Sundance chapter in the book you're reading.

1500 hours I got a visit from my fellow lookout friend, Chuck Petty, and he was bearing a wonderful gift…SALT! I had just casually mentioned—during their flight—that I was out of salt. I couldn't believe my eyes when he handed it to me.

🐿 Day 40

My lookout neighbors, Pam on Indian Mountain, and Carol on Gisborne, are down off their towers, making the airwaves kind of quiet this morning. Also gone are my Rocky's from the mountaintop, my Golden Mantled ground squirrel buddies hidden in their burrows for a long nine-month nap.

Also gone are all the snacks that John and Donna left yesterday. They lasted only a couple hours.

1000 hours   I was sitting on the east side of the catwalk, hearing this chirping/screeching sound of my golden eagle neighbors. I looked out over Lost Creek and saw the two huge birds flying about the same elevation as the tower. I quickly grabbed my camera and clicked off a couple of pictures of the beautiful birds of prey to prove to Judy that I wasn't just making up these eagle sightings. Later on today I had plans of hiking out to Eagle Mount to see if I could maybe spot them close up and personal.

1100 hours   *Na na na naing* came from close by. I looked up to see a red-breasted nuthatch on the northeast corner of the catwalk, eating bugs. Then it flew up on the 2x10 pulley overhang, eating some more bugs, before flying off.

1330 hours   A military helicopter flies by the lookout at eye level. I waved to the people inside who I could see waving back. A little excitement on this glorious Indian Summer day. I watch the large green helicopter melt into the rugged Selkirk Crest.

In the book *Lost on the Appalachian Trail* that I'm reading, the author, Kyle Rohrig, calls it Trail Magic when somebody helps you out by giving you a ride to town, or handing out cold beverages, giving you a place to stay for the night, or has you over for a meal. Well, I've been getting some Lookout Magic up here on Sundance. Yesterday I got a bunch of snacks. Today Peter Smith and Robert Benson, who gave me some chocolate the other day, were back up here on motorcycles, bearing more gifts. This time it was a ham and cheese sandwich, a huge Hershey's chocolate bar, M&M's, and a Milky Way! They had said they'd be back with some more goodies and they delivered!

1430 hours   A smoke appears off to the southwest. I spring into action, getting an azimuth on the Osborne Firefinder—217 degrees and 20 minutes, and a legal description of Section 17, Township 58 North, Range 4 West, about two miles southwest of Whitetail Butte. I call it into Dispatch, adding that it appears to be somebody burning because it puffs up really good then dies back down like they're throwing more wood on the fire. They said to let them know if it really starts smoking. It felt good to report a smoke again, even though it wasn't a wildfire.

1700 hours   I grab my daypack with water, chocolate bars, first-aid kit, Forest Radio, extra jacket, and toilet paper, lock the catwalk gate and head out on a much-looked-forward-to hike to Eagle Mount. With virtually no trails into the backcountry I went cross-country, past the pika perch, negotiating down the steep rock-strewn slope to the huckleberry patch, then along the flat grassy land bridge to the rocky knob that overlooks the granite rock wall, when I suddenly realized something. Thick in the middle of grizzly country, I realized that I forgot my bear spray! Big mistake! I had seen the video that a hunter took in the backcountry of a grizzly a couple years ago. Also I had heard report after report of people seeing them in this country! I had visions of running into a mad grizzly with only the protection of a 3" folding Buck knife I had. Not good. I said a little prayer that I wouldn't cross paths with the top of the food chain, then dove off the rock outcrop and negotiated the rock strewn slope to my destination. Down I went, carefully going over and around the large rocks until I got to a saddle, where I saw some old moose droppings. Then I climbed up the spine of the ridge until I found the most perfect sitting rock just below the west end of Eagle Mount. Setting my butt down, I took up my vigil for seeing any eagles or my furry little rock rabbit pika companions. While eating a Milky Way I gazed back at the tower a mile away. The whole north and northeast side of the lookout had an extremely steep rocky slope where probably no person in their right mind had ever gone. Below me and to the east under the rock wall that loomed over my head, was a huge boulder field where also no one would want to venture. Deep in the alpine cirque below the boulders was a small grassy flat which was surrounded by the hardest, rock-strewn country you could imagine getting through. The only easy way to get to the open ridgerunning farther to the east, was to hike right up against the rock wall that loomed above my head. I knew it because I had hiked it a couple years ago. I did a pika imitation to get the party started. Immediately I got a response. Then another imitation was followed by a chorus of *eeeeks*. I washed the chocolate bar down with some water from my Nalgene bottle and listened to some more pikas calling out. I kept my ears tuned to hear some eagle screeches too, but didn't catch anything to announce their presence. Then suddenly, twenty feet below me, I saw a little rock rabbit scurry across a boulder. I stayed glued to my seat, listening to more *eeeeks* over the next forty-five minutes. Even though I didn't hear or see my golden eagle neighbors, I was convinced that they had a nest in amongst these rock walls. Hoping I wouldn't run into a griz on the way back, I quickly scrambled up the steep rocky mountainside, back to my home in the sky.

🌲 *October 2nd*

1230 hours   Pam Aunan, the Indian Mountain Lookout and good friend of mine, shows up for a visit, bringing snacks and fruit and juice which would get me through my last four days of the season. We spent a couple hours sitting out on the catwalk and talking about the plane flight with pilot Chuck. We also talked about her old lookout home on Lookout Mountain, chatting about her time on Indian Mountain Lookout, and about my life up here on Sundance. We were treated with seeing a golden eagle soaring over the lookout. It was the fastest two hours of just soaking up the sunshine and being with my friend on the lookout.

1505 hours   The airwaves come alive with Engine 1151 heading to the report of a fire in the Two Mouth area. I take a quick check of the area far off to the north and can't find anything, which is good. The fire season *isn't* quite over yet.

1545 hours   Engine 1151 reports to Dispatch that they are at the Last Day Fire, an escaped campfire at $1/10^{th}$ acre and that they can handle it.

🌲 Day 44

Two days until the end of my stay on Sundance, and I'm getting sad to leave, but it will be good to be back with Judy. Yesterday was a busy day. I had 34 people visiting Sundance. Hikers, picnickers, and folks who climbed the tower. I even had two people who got engaged up here on the mountain. Kerry and Chris Bradley, from Spokane, had the big event at the Sundance Memorial sign. I wished them the very best in their married lives. I even talked about some of my experiences in the area near Indian Hill to some visitors. I told them about the cougar that I nearly walked up to a few hundred feet from the lookout. How it came out onto the road near me when I was coming back to the tower on a morning walk. I'll never forget the loud scream it let out before slinking off the ridge towards the water trail. And I told the Sundance visitors that on another morning walk I almost bumped into a sleeping black bear, that fortunately high-tailed away from me when I woke it up. I also related the story about the time in 1975 when I was hiking back from Otter Butte, and got caught in a snowstorm. Dead tired, wet and cold, and very hypothermic from climbing 4,000 vertical feet out of Otter Creek, I lay down in the snow and fell asleep. Suddenly I woke up from what I thought was a dream of Judy calling out to me in the fog, over two miles away. Getting up, I hiked ever so slowly but surely, back to the lookout. My wife had saved my life. Filled with the stories of close encounters I had at my old summer Indian Hill home, the visitors left the mountaintop—a trip I think they will never forget.

1610 hours   Out to the west I see my golden eagle neighbor flying about 1,000 feet over the ridge. I quickly grab my binoculars and follow him in flight…soaring out over Lee Creek, then Lost Creek. I get such a wonderful feeling of freedom as I stay glued to the 12x50 Bushnell's, following the bird of prey until he disappears in the distance.

I learn from a visitor that Eagle Mount is called an arete, where glaciers formed on both sides of the rock wall.

🐝 Day 45

0815 hours   On my walkabout this morning I chose to go to the top of the bluff to the southwest of the tower, through the snag patch to absorb the beautifully calm, blue-sky day. I sat on a rock ledge and peered over to Sundance through the 1967 Fire Whitebark Pine snags, which gave me my favorite view of the lookout tower. Suddenly, an unidentified gray bird about the size of a robin comes flying my way, until he lands on the same rock ledge I'm on just two feet away! Talk about being one with nature, the bird never saw me as a threat until I flinched and scared it away.

Back at the lookout I did a quick survey of my supplies after more than six weeks of living up here without a resupply. The freezer was empty, the cupboard was bare. Gone was the hot chocolate. Gone was the tea. Gone was the oatmeal, the popcorn, the Wheat Thins, the potato chips, the chocolate bars, the peanut butter, the powdered lemonade, and the huckleberries and pancake mix. Last night's supper was a Mountain House freeze-dried meal. Thankfully I still had the sausage and pineapple juice that Pam brought. I'm going to limp to the finish line and just have enough food to get me through.

My second to last day's entertainment is watching the chipmunks scurry from rock to rock. Gone from the mountaintop are all the ground squirrels and I haven't seen the blue grouse for days.

1600 hours   With a cold wind blowing at a good 20 mph out on the catwalk, I move my operations inside, reading Jerry Ellis' book, *Bareback*, about the Pony Express Trail, in the cushy chair at the table where I write and eat, soaking up the warmth of the sun. I am also soaking up the awesomeness of the Selkirk Crest, looming off to my northeast, my favorite view. Their craggy crests dominate the skyline; Roman Nose, Hunt Peak, Gunsight Peak, Bottleneck Mountain, Twin Peaks, Chimney Rock, Mount Roothaan, the Wigwams, and Lion's Head. I can't get enough of them, but soon they will be just a memory when I leave for my other home in Montana tomorrow. I will miss them like best friends. I will miss the golden eagles, the chipmunks, the Golden Mantled and Columbian ground squirrels, and the grouse as they do tours of the mountaintop. I will miss the Blue Angels of yet unidentified little gray-white birds doing strafing runs on the lookout. I will miss the mule deer as they make their way through my lookout yard. I will miss the star shows, and the moon as it moves across the night sky. I will miss the awesome sunrises over Montana and the equally impressive sunsets out over Washington. I will miss seeing all 19 miles of the beautiful Priest Lake every day. And I will miss long-eyeing the mountains on my horizon: Snowshoe Peak, 60 miles away in the Cabinet Range in Montana, Clifty Peak far off to my east, Snowy Top Mountain by the border, the Canadian Rockies beyond that, the mystery lookout in Canada, and the Colville Mountains far off to my west, over 80 miles away. I will miss popcorn night on Wednesdays. I will miss making huckleberry pancakes on Saturday mornings. I will miss being on the lookout searching for any hint of smoke that would trigger me into action to plot it on the Osborne Firefinder and call it into Coeur d'Alene Dispatch. I will miss hiking out to Eagle Mount. I will miss my walkabouts in the morning. And I will miss singing John Denver songs and the Sound of Music when I am washing dishes while looking out at all this incredible scenery.

1715 hours   I lock the catwalk gate, climb down the 46 steps and hike on the path that leads me east towards the pika perch. Tonight's hike, though, is taking me up and over the rock outcrop and I scramble down a steep, rocky slope to the Geo-Cache to leave a goodbye note. It takes me a little while to find it, but then I discover the military green ammo can hidden underneath some huge slabs of rock. I grab the can and open it up to get the notebook that 59 other people have signed since 2003. The last entry in the book...

This is my 45th year on lookout- 35 years on Indian Hill in the Nez Perce Forest, and 10 years on Sundance. Missed last year because I had Lymphoma Cancer. Now in remission, I'm so glad to be back up here as the "closer". Had a huge windstorm on Labor Day. Over 80 mph wind gusts. Found the Blanchard Fire—it got to be over 600 acres. This is my favorite spot to come and listen for the eeeeks of the pikas in the scree slope. Till next year...

Climbing back up to the pika perch, it's the perfect place to sit on the last night of my lookout season on Sundance. I've got a great view of the open, huckleberry ridge that leads to the rock outcrop where I had seen the two golden eagles earlier in the year land on top of Eagle Mount. My view of Eagle Mount from here is impressive. Across Soldier Creek I can see acres and acres of aspens turning golden. A large stand of larch trees is also turning golden off to my northeast. I can hear my favorite little pika friends below me. I like the idea that probably no person has ever set foot where the pikas live. Right now I know that they are busy making tiny haystacks for the long winter ahead.

Tomorrow I'll start my rig up, and for the first time in 46 days, drive down the steep, narrow lookout road back to civilization. I'll miss all my neighbors. And I will especially miss the pikas off this perch. But all fall, winter and spring I'll look forward to once again living the Sundance Lookout experience.

So long, Sundance...

Pikas are my favorite little furry creatures up on Sundance

Sundance Lookout

My new home since 2010

Above: At the lookout sign with Mount Roothaan in the distance

On catwalk with Priest Lake in the background

Osborne firefinder at Sundance

The new Sundance Fire sign that Jackson Conlin (right) built with help by Tyler Zandhuisen (left)

The Selkirk Crest

Priest River Valley filled with fog

My favorite hiking area near the lookout

"Eagle Mount"

The view of Sundance from "Eagle Mount"

Below: Chuck Petty — a fellow volunteer lookout at Sundance

Above: Pictured L to R: Tyler Zandhuisen, Jackson Conlin, and Scott Cordes, the Priest Lake fire crew, heading out to the Lookout John Fire

Above: Looking north over Priest Lake and into Canada

A piece of charred wood from the Lookout John Fire

End of season snowstorm

Afterword

I thought the Sundance story was finished, until I got the biggest lightning storm I'd ever been in up here on September 12th, 2021. Sitting on my lightning chair, I saw strike after strike hit the lookout ridge, even slamming twice into the tower. Twenty minutes of this heavenly barrage, I peered out of my east-side windows and immediately saw a nice little candle glow coming from below a talus slope at the foot of Eagle Mount. Hallelujah. I found a fire! I quickly aimed the firefinder on the only fire I'd ever seen near Sundance. After calling it in to Coeur d'Alene Dispatch, it was like the calvary responded, the Priest Lake Fire Crew coming up to get a bead on it. By 2200 hours the troops had arrived! Standing out on the catwalk, Tyler Zandhuisen, Scott Cordes, Colter Lee, and Jackson Conlin, took turns staring at it through binoculars, watching the lone tree shoot embers into the night. Giving me the word that they'd attack it in the morning, they left the lookout for the ranger station.

After an unsuccessful attempt to attack it from the road in Soldier Creek the next day, Tyler, Scott, and Jackson came back to the lookout on the 14th bright and early, to hike a mile and a half into the rugged backcountry to try and find it. I cheered the fire crew on, as single file they went out to scramble over and around huge rocks and boulders and crash through the brush down the steep mountainslopes, loaded down with fire packs, chainsaw, pulaskis, and shovel. Reality struck home as my credibility as a lookout was on the line! Leading a crew into a fire that is showing smoke is one thing. But leading the crew in to a fire that *isn't* showing smoke is quite another thing. I had a distinct memory that the fire was about 50 yards beneath the talus slope below Eagle Mount. I prayed that my memory would serve me well and they'd find my smoke-less fire.

Patiently I waited at the lookout until the radio came alive with the fire crew asking if I could see them. Looking through binoculars I immediately saw the red-hardhatted crew on the boulders above the location of the fire. "You need to go downhill about 50 yards on that spur ridge in front of you."

I had studied this fire yesterday and had found another *key* landmark to help lead them into it...a large white slab of bedrock, about 25 yards directly to the east that was almost directly in line with the fire. I zoomed in on the three crewmen with my Bushnells, watching them scour the mountainside beneath the talus slope. I waited until they were almost even with that white rock. "You guys are in the right area!" I announced over IDL Direct 4, the secondary channel.

"We found it!" I heard Tyler immediately exclaim.

"You guys are great fire finders!" I gleefully announced over the air.

"*You* are a great fire finder!" they responded.

Then the best was yet to come. After they asked me what I'd like to name the fire, I thought for a moment and said, "The Lookout John Fire."

In 46 years of being a fire lookout, it was my proudest moment when they called in to Coeur d'Alene Dispatch and officially announced that it was The Lookout John Fire! I was beaming with pride up at Sundance, so glad that I could lead them into a fire that wasn't showing even a hint of smoke after burning for 48 hours.

After the crew put out the fire and made the tough hike back to the lookout, I had three ice-cold Mountain Dews waiting for them. We all toasted to each other for a job well done. Then they told me that they were really glad that I was the Sundance Lookout. After trading notes about the fire, they left me with a souvenir...a piece of charred wood that they had brought back. After they left I wrote in capital letters in pencil on it—FROM LOOKOUT JOHN FIRE TO THE EAST OF SUNDANCE. DISCOVERED 9-12-21. A momento that will always be on the shelf above the west bank of windows at Sundance Lookout.

Epilogue

It had been just two weeks since I came down from Sundance and I was already itching to get up high again. Judy was a couple hundred feet ahead of me as I rounded the last steep switchback on our annual hike up to Skookum Butte Lookout, a log lookout built in 1928, and recently restored to its original condition. The relatively short but extremely steep mountain trail always kicked my butt, as I huffed and puffed my way to tie in with my hiking buddy at the base of the huge rock-strewn slope that surrounded the white-painted lookout like a mote around a castle. Judy followed the trail to the south that wound its way up to the 7,215-foot summit, while I stayed behind staring up at the lookout. It had been three years since our last climb to the top of the butte, the pilgrimage canceled when I was having chemo treatments for my cancer in 2019.

It was an appropriate place to go to end my lookout book, at a fire lookout on the Idaho/Montana state line, high above the Lolo Creek valley. As it usually did, the wind swept over the rocky ridge that the log cabin lookout sat on, reminding me of the strong winds up on Sundance. I took off my daypack and tore into it to get part of my lunch—a Hershey's Bar—to replenish some of the energy that I used to reach the peak. The view was grand! We gazed out from the lookout ridge... the jagged crest of the Bitterroots to our southeast, Lolo Peak standing tall just off to our east; the 10,000-foot high Mission Mountains far off to our northeast; the Lolo Creek valley to our north, with tens of thousands of golden larch trees aflame in the East Fork; the mountains of the Great Burn wilderness far off to our northwest; the Selway Crags melting into the distance to our west; Ranger Peak standing tall off to our south, past Beaver Ridge. Then I took out the binoculars from my pack and zero'd in on the fire lookouts that I could see from Skookum—Stark Mountain, White Mountain, Rocky Point, Bear Mountain, Grave's Peak, and Beaver Ridge. Judy and I checked on the restoration project, finding only the north side left to restore.

Amongst the grandeur of the mountains, and in the wind-shadow on the east side of the log lookout, we ate our lunch, and stared out at Lolo Peak and the extent of the 2017 Lolo Peak Fire, which threatened our home and led to an evacuation. It burned over 50,000 acres, a lot of it that we could see as we munched on our store-bought hoagie sandwiches.

I felt at peace, as I usually did with Judy, gazing out at the sawtoothed Bitterroot Divide from the butte. It resurrected memories of our time up on Indian Hill, spending our summers together, being a lookout team on the mountaintop from 1974 through 1994, some of the best years of my life.

It has been a way of life for me for 46 years now. And I plan on going up to Sundance for as long as I am able…to again be on top of the world!

Return to Indian Hill

🌲 *June 22nd, 2022*

    I'm sitting here, suspended 41 feet above the Earth, in an all-glass house that is smaller than most people's bedrooms, and loving every minute of being back at my beloved Indian Hill Lookout! Thanks to Jon Norman, the Fire Management Officer, and Ryan Nuxoll, the Assistant Fire Management Officer of the Moose Creek District, I have returned for eight wonderful days to be the fire spotter from high above the Selway River that winds like a huge slithering snake off to the north of the tower.

    It was a reunion with an "old friend" that I'd been looking forward to ever since I left in September of 2008. Andrew, Mitch, and Kelley of the fire crew helped raise the shutters. After they left, the curtain of fog that hung over the mountaintop finally lifted, which led to an "Oh my God" moment—the whole southern part of the mountaintop was completely open now, its thick tree cover completely slicked off from the 2015 Wash Fire that consumed what the Slims Fire didn't burn. And another "Oh my God" moment was seeing all the snow that still covered the mountaintop—more than I had ever seen in late June. With the tree cover gone on the west side of the ridge, a massive 25-foot deep cornice developed on the east side of the Indian Hill Ridge. When the fog completely broke apart, all the high country was exposed, still laden with a thick blanket of snow. The Selway Crags were totally buried, as was all the higher terrain off to my east in the wilderness—Copper Butte, Little Copper Butte, Vermilion Peak, Indian Peak, and the Buck Lake Ridge, completely white.

    My job of being a lookout, is always to keep a constant vigil for forest fires from my high perch. So far all I'm seeing is pollen dust drifting off of the tops of the trees that looks suspiciously like smoke—but not to this fire spotter of 47 years. Even though it's been a wet spring, I still keep a close watch for any lightning holdover fires that might be smoldering, waiting for a good wind to bring them back to life. And that's what the wind is doing right now, gusting up to at least 25 mph out of the west. Time for another fire scan and then back to washing the windows.

"*Ouchhh!*" I had to pinch myself to see if this was truly real, or *just* a dream, of my being up on Indian Hill all by my lonesome. Yes, it surely is real! Halfway through the window-washing job (80 panes in all), it's time for a slush break. So I grabbed my Sierra Cup, climbed down the four flights of stairs and dug into the closest patch of snow, about twenty feet from the tower, and filled my cup with the frozen treat. Better than anything at DQ, I'm sitting back in my captain's chair on the east side of the catwalk—with sunshine on my shoulders—gazing out across the million acres of the Selway Bitterroot Wilderness, and enjoying the snow cone in a cup. How could life get any better?

1630 hours   With the windows finally cleaned I can see forever!

I've come up with a plan...use snow, in addition to going to the lower spring for water. So I filled a large stainless-steel bowl and pot with snow and set them out in the sun on the catwalk to melt. It *was* a good plan except for all the bugs that got into the snowmelt out on the catwalk. So I dug up some more snow and put it inside the lookout like I should have done in the first place.

Tonight's entrée...Freeze-dried Beef Stroganoff with Noodles, a Mountain House favorite of mine. For my 8 day stay up here up on the lookout, it will be like I'm backpacking, with all my gear brought up in my Kelty pack. It will be the same pack, with the same Mountain House cuisine I'll have when my friend, Gary Winek and I backpack in the Crags at the end of July, between my Indian Hill and Sundance stints. I'm just hoping, as I stare out of my newly cleaned windows, that the alpine lakes we plan to camp at will be ice free so that we can catch nice succulent trout for a lot of our meals.

1703 hours   Just checked in to Grangeville Dispatch, almost goofing up and saying "Couer d' Alene Dispatch" and calling myself "Sundance Lookout". It's super neat to know that I'm the *opener* on Indian Hill and the *closer* on Sundance.

Except for the three years that we got helicoptered up here in the 1970s, I've never felt so remote on lookout. Left off by the fire crew who brought me up on an all-terrain vehicle, I'm afoot now. The road, with more slough-offs on the downhill sides than I could count, is impassable to pickups or SUV's. Only narrow-wheel-based 4-wheelers have a shot at making it past the slides. And I like this feeling of being isolated, alone on top of a mountaintop to spend a week, reliving the 35 years that I spent up here in paradise. Up at dawn, I go on my morning water hauls, walking down the road to the lower spring. Disappointingly I can't find the spring trail in all the blowdown from the burn. I check out the tracks from the nightly deer and elk visitors. Some trips down I see who left those tracks, watching the mule deer watching me. And—after work hours—I go visit old haunts...lying down in the large meadow where I went to get flowers for Judy on our anniversaries that we spent together up here; checking out the meadow a quarter mile down the Copper Butter Trail; hiking the open ridge to the southeast and checking out the Patrol Point, where I can peer down into Bluff Creek at the two rock cairns; climbing to the highest part of the Indian Hill Ridge and seeing into the Meadow Creek backcountry that is blocked by the knob; checking out the hunter camps a couple hundred yards to the south. But my favorite hike, where I used to go with Fritz to the top of the bluffs just to the southeast of the tower, is—due to safety concerns—off limits to me now. The huge, nearly mile long cornice that clings to the ridge, is impossible to navigate to get to the bluff overlook. So I'll have to be satisfied just looking at the special place from the lookout.

The new view to the south of the tower, that kind of shocked me when I first saw it on my first day, is growing on me. At first I was dismayed at seeing all those lodgepoles and alpine firs totally gone, but the meadow that replaced it is quite beautiful, and is a lot easier to hike through now. It looks like a great area to spot deer and elk from the tower.

It warms my heart to watch my Columbian Ground Squirrel neighbors playing chase in the lookout yard, and gathering up grass for their underground nests. Missing, though, are the Golden Mantled Ground Squirrels that I had all named Rocky. Ravens, hawks, and eagles soar over the ridge, as I gaze out at them through my lookout windows. I've heard the heavenly notes of the "lark of the mountain", and the "echo bird". And swallows still divebomb the lookout. But sadly missing since my arrival 5 days ago are the gray jays that I used to call and have them eat right out of my hand.

Corral Hill, Shissler Peak and Indian Hill are the only lookouts up on the Forest (I was officially the first lookout up. Other lookouts are waiting for the snow to melt back so that they can get up to their respective lookouts. A couple days ago I heard the unmistakable voice of Gary Dutcher over the airwaves. I'm sure he's anxiously waiting for his road to clear of snow so that he can get up to his lookout on Pilot Knob that's been his summer home for decades.

A quick survey of the log cabin when we arrived showed that the Indian Hill sign was missing. The winter wasn't too kind, as the support to hold up the sign was broken off, and one of the flagpole supports had split in two, another winter casualty.

With all the snow up here, its made for some interesting walking in the area. I have to walk on snow when I go to the outhouse, I go over snow when I go to the spring, and I can't help but walk over the safer west side of the cornice out Indian Hill Ridge. I've fallen through the snow in many hollow spots, and I've slid on the steeper sloped snowbanks when I didn't want to.

🌲 Day 5

I headed out from the tower at the crack of dawn, on a mission...to finally locate the spring trail because I was tired of hiking the three mile round trip on the road to the lower spring. I kind of had given up on finding it due to the excessive amount of downfall from the Wash Creek Fire. But not today. With my two backpacking Nalgene bottles in hand, I made my way past the log cabin, skirting the huge corniced snowbank on the east side of the ridge, and made my way up the road to where the trail took off. I scoured the area, with no luck. Then I just took off, traversing the area until I found the slight depression of a trail that looked so familiar from years of using it. But this was where the mystery came in. I knew that the trail forked about 200 feet from the road, one heading to the meadow and the cut-off trail going to the upper and lower springs. With it all open now and downed trees everywhere, it all looked so different. But not all *that* different! I remembered that once you left the meadow trail, the country got a lot steeper and you hiked down just to the west of a draw. Bingo! I followed my instincts and dropped off of the ridge, finally finding the trench of a trail that indeed was following the slight crease in the mountain. Down I went, up and over downed burnt logs lacing the trail. It was like old times, when I'd go for water on this path, sometimes taking my little buddy, Fritz. *Movement* ahead! Then snorting. I stopped on a dime and saw two mule deer, one 4-point buck in velvet, and a doe. The doe bounded off, but the buck stood his ground, staring at me. We stared at each other for a few minutes, then he took off, joining the doe across the slope. As I continued on my way on the old familiar trail, I began to hear water trickling from the draw on my left. Veering off the trail, I soon got to a narrow chute of water falling over a ledge, a perfect spot to fill up. I recalled many times filling up here in the early part of the season in good snow years. Above me a 15-foot high cornice hugged the leeward side of the meadow trail ridge. A couple hundred yards shy of the upper spring, I now had a lot shorter of a hike back up to the lookout.

If things couldn't get any better this morning, when I arrived back on the mountaintop my heart was filled with joy when I saw a bunch of colorful phlox blooming just south of the helispot. I naturally got down on all fours and sniffed the heavenly alpine aroma. Now I had two colorful flowers adorning the mountaintop...the phlox and the glacier lilies that followed the receding snowbanks.

Being on Indian Hill now is about as good as being on a wilderness lookout. Hardly a soul is attempting this marginal road. In the nearly a week since I arrived, I've only had a few people up here. And I love it...the feeling of truly being isolated from civilization, and without transportation. Yes... this is my cup of tea!

Besides looking out for fires every twenty minutes, I'm keeping busy with little projects. Besides washing all the windows, I've cleaned the sills, kept the floor swept, cleaned the firefinder map, chopped firewood, scraped paint on the stairway railings, mucked out the log cabin and nailed up the 2-legged table to the south wall, wired up the split flagpole support post, and shored up a broken boardwalk board with a firewood round. I definitely want to be "earning my keep" up here.

I spend some time going over my maps, relearning the

many tributaries of the Selway. I stop my scan of the immense country at an obscure, but very beautiful drainage—Ballinger Creek. What draws me to it every day are all the cascading falls—about a mile in length—that shows up as a bright, sun-reflected, ribbon of white in the otherwise green scene. The falls are nearly inaccessible, being a good four brushy, rattlesnake-infested miles away from the river trail. A neat thought enters my mind that maybe nobody has ever seen these cascading falls "on the ground".

🐝 Day 6

1533 hours   I stare out of my windows at a raven flying out over Bluff Creek, doing aerial acrobatics to his very entertained lookout audience. I watch it as he melts into the southern horizon, disappearing from view.

Still no people visitors for a Saturday. I am loving this peace and quiet on lookout. A half an hour later I am eating my words as Ashlee and Jesse show up in a side-by-side, from O'Hara Campground on the Selway.

The rushing sound of snowmelt cascading off slabs of rock down in Bluff Creek drifts up to my lookout perch. On Day 3 it was that sound that lured me down there to get my daily supply of water. I had studied the best route down to where I could see the reflection of a tiny snowmelt stream source, and headed for it. What looked easy from the tower wasn't that easy on the ground. As steep as a cow's face, I kept the brakes on as I cautiously descended towards the perched basin at my feet. Soon I got to some old snowdrifts that I kicked steps in to get across. Continuing my way down, I arrived at a beautiful snow-free green avenue, which led me to the little stream I'd seen from the tower. I quenched my thirst first before topping off my water bottles, then sat down on a log and took in the view. Just above my head was this strange scene. A big circle of snow melted out, forming a frame around a large rock. Beautiful trilliums and glacier lilies filled the small grassy meadow that I was in. Arching my neck to the west, I saw the top half of the lookout staring down at me. And I checked out the impressive cornice along the ridge. Snorting coming from off to my north, I saw two mule deer bounding up the 100% slope to escape this intruder. I took another swig from my water bottle and began the steep ascent back home. I followed my boot prints across the snow and crashed through alder brush to get to the steep, grassy chute that I had come down. My winter's workout program wasn't helping much, as I struggled to climb what was so easy to descend. One rest break after another, I inched my way next to these towering bluffs, slipping about every third step on the extremely steep slope. By the time that I got to the top of the ridge—after about ten rest stops—I almost had one whole Nalgene bottle of water consumed. Lucky that I had the two bottles. Back on top of the tower, breathing hard after that tough climb, I peered over the railing at that little paradise below me. I was glad to have gone down there, but would probably never go down there for water again.

Day 7

0400 hours   I wake from a dream to a picture perfect celestial scene out of my east windows. A waning crescent moon and Venus are shining bright above the deep amber glow of the sun silhouetting the jagged crest of the Bitterroot Divide. I sit up on my lookout bed, taking in the spectacular sight.

On my early morning water haul I get another wonderful treat as the "lark of the mountain" serenades me, singing this beautiful song over and over. The "lark" flies off to a different snag and continues his concert.

The Wash Fire of 2015 almost burned down the lookout. Burning the lower portions of two tower legs, the east-side diagonal braces, three sets of cross braces, the lower part of the stairway, and most of the boardwalk. Indian Hill Lookout almost wasn't left standing. For years after 2015, the lookout was not staffed...until a very talented work crew came up here and totally repaired it. Treated 8x8's were spliced to the bottom part of the north-side legs. The burnt cross braces and diagonal braces were replaced with treated timbers. The boardwalk replaced. Concrete footings for the northeast tower leg and the stairway were constructed. Even the lower part of the stairway railings were replaced. As a carpenter myself, I applaud their efforts. They did one heck of a good job!

0825 hours   Hallelujah! A Rocky sighting! At first I thought I was seeing things, but no—this is the real deal—there's a Golden Mantled ground squirrel scampering around down in the rocks below the tower! Too bad that I don't have any pancakes to feed him.

My time up here on Indian Hill now is whittled down to less than 24 hours. By this time tomorrow I will have handed off the baton to Cori Nease for the rest of the fire season, and will be headed down the road with the fire crew. I can't remember when something meant so much to me than this reunion with an "old friend".

This place was my home for 35 wonderful years. All the varnished laminated wood cabinet tops and firefinder cabinet that I made, the catwalk gate that I constructed, all the west-side windows that I built from scratch down at the ranger station and installed. And especially the woodstove that I installed in 1993, and brought bucket after bucket full of mortar up the tower to make the hearth. And that's where this lookout story will end as I lean over and read the names that are etched in the mortar around a slab of rock that's in the shape of the state of Idaho. It has all our names; John and Judy, Fritz, Rhoda and Fluffy, bringing back all those wonderful years that we had up here on Indian Hill. This has been the culmination of a wonderful week to reminisce about the "good old days".

It was a dream come true to come back up here as the official Indian Hill Lookout for a week. The best thing would be to know that I could do it all over again next fire season. My wish came true when I got the word that I would be coming back in June of 2023 to again open the lookout for the fire season, to again be *Above It All...*

Post Script

On October 11th, 2022, when I was looking through my emails after coming down off of Sundance Lookout for the season, I discovered one from Cheryl Hogan, the Lead Fire Dispatcher out of Coeur d'Alene. It was a simple message, but one that packed a huge punch...she had called me "Eagle Eye John"! I had just come off of a 49 day stint on Sundance Lookout, where I had spotted and reported 14 wildland fires, 4 of which were way up in Canada—including at least one that the Canadian government didn't even know about! In the 47 years that I've been a fire lookout, that indeed was the highest compliment I've ever received. And on October 3rd, I got a real treat when my publisher Rachel Burk and her husband Joe, came up to Sundance for a visit. Like it couldn't have been timed any better, as soon as they climbed to the top of the tower, the two resident golden eagles showed up, soaring high over Lost Creek, entertaining their audience out on the south side of the catwalk. Just before Rachel's Dad, Dale, passed away in 2020, I had given him a call and described to him about the resident golden eagles that I had seen up at Sundance. His interest was immediately lit, telling me how much he loved golden eagles. I found it fitting that his daughter could see the eagles that I told her Dad about.

Top and Middle photos: Golden Eagles soaring above Lost Creek

Rachel and Joe at Sundance Lookout 2022

Mitch Erie, Andrew Bertels and Kelly Harkins of the fire crew who took me up to Indian Hill on June 20, 2022

Cori Nease, current Indian Hill lookout and his dog Teddy

Snowfield on Indian Hill on June 23, 2022

Mile long, 25-foot deep cornice along Indian Hill Ridge

Author scanning the forest for smokes, 2022

2021 Idaho Department of Lands—Priest Lake Supervisory Area Fire Team

Dan Brown—Current Area Manager and Fire Warden from 2007-2020

Dave Thornton—Fire Warden

John Cook—Assistant Fire Warden

Fire Crew

Luke Sater

Matt Pancheri

Justin Allbee

Joe Anderson

Kase Belmont

Ed Kassa

Tyler Zandhuisen

Scott Cordes

Jackson Conlin

Colter Lee

Pam Aunan

2021 Sundance Lookouts

Emily Sparrow

Chuck Petty

Jeannie Nez Perce

Terry Thurlow

Michael Decker

Barb Conboy

Avellino and Helen Persello

John Hayes

Gerry Graszl

Stephanie Kung

Vicki Vesecky

John Crawford

John Cook, and Vicki and John's 2-month-old baby boy, Fynn Cook

2022 Moose Creek Ranger District Fire Team

Jon Norman—Fire Management Officer

Ryan Nuxoll—Assistant Fire Management Officer in Operations

Dustin Decker—Assistant Fire Management Officer in Fuels

Selway Wilderness Fire Module

JT Sohr

Nolan Buckingham

Matt Ruskey

Kelley Harkins

Camille Wood-Foucar

Ingrid Lickiss

Alan Verona

Mitch Erie

Brett Raymond

Amber Langley

Engine Crew

Nathan Seitz

John Link

Robert Ramont

Timothy Damann

Tyler Martin—Fuels Tech

Cash Rubelt

Andrew Bertels

Daniel Velasco

Adrian Jimenez

Lookouts

Indian Hill—Cori Nease and John Crawford

Coolwater—Tom Vandewater

Shissler—Evelyn Genadek

Corral Hill—Kevin Roach

Gardiner—Lisa Buchanan

ADVENTURE AWAITS...

Author, John Crawford, is seen here in Sheep Canyon on the Mickelson Trail in the Black Hills of South Dakota on a week-long mountain biking adventure. His next book, **Adventure Awaits**, will be a collection of his adventures in snowshoeing, kayaking, canoeing, mountain biking, backpacking, and mountain climbing across this country. Five of the stories are with his friend, Gary Winek, and the rest are solo treks. Also included is a harrowing story of his Dad's nighttime sailboat race across Lake Michigan.

BOOKS BY JOHN CRAWFORD

To purchase these books, please contact the author at:
lookoutjohn51@gmail.com
John's books can also be found at several retailers in Montana and Idaho, and can also be purchased direct from Stoneydale Press Publishing at 406-777-2729.

Milky Way as seen from Sundance Lookout
Photo by Gerry Graszl